Science Skills Builder

How Science Works, Maths in Science and Quality of Written Communication

MARK LEVESLEY

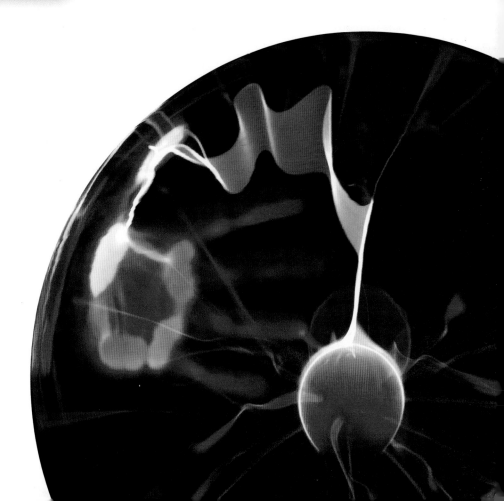

Published by Collins
An imprint of HarperCollinsPublishers
77–85 Fulham Palace Road
Hammersmith
London
W6 8JB

Browse the complete Collins catalogue at:
www.collinseducation.com

© HarperCollinsPublishers Limited 2012

10 9 8 7 6 5 4 3 2

ISBN-13 978 0 00 745725 0

Mark Levesley asserts his moral right to be identified as the author of this work.

British Library Cataloguing in Publication Data
A Catalogue record for this publication is available from the British Library

Commissioned by Letitia Luff
Proofread by Joan Miller
Indexed by INDEXING SPECIALISTS (UK) Ltd.
Designed and Project managed by Ken Vail Graphic Design
Illustrations by Ken Vail Graphic Design, Phill Burrows and Beehive Illustration (Laslo Veres)
Picture research by Grace Glendinning
Concept design by Anna Plucinska
Cover design by Julie Martin
Production by Rebecca Evans

Printed in China

MIX
Paper from
responsible sources
FSC
www.fsc.org
FSC™ C007454

Credits
Thanks to Lucy English, Chris Pearce and Ed Walsh for their reviews.

Acknowledgements
The publishers wish to thank the following for permission to reproduce photographs. Every effort has been made to trace copyright holders and to obtain their permission for the use of copyright materials. The publishers will gladly receive any information enabling them to rectify any error or omission at the first opportunity.

Photo credits
The publisher would like to thank the following for permission to reproduce pictures in these pages.

(t = top, b = bottom, c = centre, l = left, r = right):

COVER Nikolay Petkov/Shutterstock, p 6 Wronkiew/WikiMedia Commons, p 7t Mikaela/Shutterstock, p 7c william casey/Shutterstock, p 8tl Photo of Anne Rooney © Anne Rooney, taken by Luki Sumner, House of Sharps and used with permission, p 8tr Cover of Drop Dead, Gorgeous used with the permission of Ransom Publishing Ltd., p 8cr Dolledre/WikiMedia Commons, p 8cl The Sydenham Society/Google Books, p 9 Peter Ommundsen, p 10r Four Oaks/Shutterstock, p 10l School of Law, University of Portsmouth, p 14t Comstock Images/Getty Images, p 14c James Heilman, MD/WikiMedia Commons, p 18t Gravicapa/Shutterstock, p 18c Andrew Lambert Photography/Science Photo Library, p 19 kristian sekulic/iStockphoto, p 20 Ramon L. Farinos/Shutterstock, p 22t PRHaney/WikiMedia Commons, p 22c JPL/NASA, p 25r Perry Harmon/Shutterstock, p 25l Chris Turner/Shutterstock, p 26 Diego Barbieri/Shutterstock, p 28 Philippe Gontier/Eurelios/Science Photo Library, p 32l Andrew Lambert Photography/Science Photo Library, p 32r Zvonimir Luketina/Shutterstock, p 35 Swapan/Shutterstock, p 39 AISPIX /Shutterstock, p 40 Comstock Images/Getty Images, p 41 Chuck Nacke/Alamy, p 46 Studio 37/Shutterstock, p 49 Robyn Mackenzie/Shutterstock, p 50t Martin Shields/Alamy, p 50b l i g h t p o e t/Shutterstock, p 50cl Toranico/Shutterstock, p 50ct wavebreakmedia ltd/Shutterstock, p 52 Chris Clinton/Getty Images, p 53l Jim Varney/ Science Photo Library, p 53t StockLite/Shutterstock, p 53br Monkey Business Images/Shutterstock, p 54 sommthink/Shutterstock, p 55c Yuri Arcurs/Shutterstock, p 55t Tyler Boyes/Shutterstock, p 55b Peter Menzel/Science Photo Library, p 56t Fiona Hanson/Press Association, p 56b Gaby Kooijman/Shutterstock, p 57 PHOTOTAKE Inc./Alamy, p 58 Catherine Yeulet/iStockphoto, p 61l Hung Chung Chih/Shutterstock, p 61r Francisco Javier Ballester Calonge/Shutterstock, p 65 Matej Hudovernik/Shutterstock, p 66c Timothy Hodgkinson/Shutterstock, p 66r Giphotostock/Science Photo Library, p 66l Giphotostock/Science Photo Library.

Contents

For the student

The reason why science is a compulsory subject for much of your time at school is because it teaches you how to think in ways that will help you throughout life. Science can be divided into two parts:

- learning about what science has already discovered
- learning about how that science was discovered (scientific skills).

Sometimes we spend too much time learning about stuff that scientists have already discovered and forget to develop our own skills of scientific discovery. It is these skills that help you to understand new technology as it becomes available, to interpret data presented on TV and the internet and to question claims made by people and advertisers.

This book is designed to help you build your confidence in using scientific skills. There's some maths too and there's also help with using English to express your scientific views and ideas clearly.

This book focuses on a range of 50 important skills. These are divided into skills needed to:

- develop ideas
- plan investigations and process data
- present data
- think about results
- understand how science is used and affects us.

Skills

In this section, the 50 core skills are explained in more detail with clear, fully illustrated explanations.

The level booster shows you how to develop your skills. It uses a star system. One star is what you should be capable of doing when you first start learning this skill. Two stars indicate what you should be able to do when you've had a bit more practice. And three stars is 'expert' level!

All the questions use the same star system that you'll find in the Level Booster boxes. So, by answering the questions and checking their answers at the back of the book, you'll be able to see the progress that you are making.

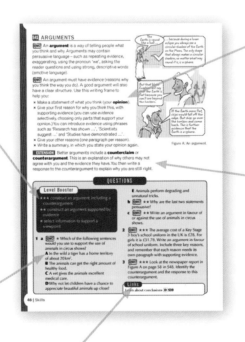

The meanings of all **bold words** in the text can be found in the glossary at the back of the book.

QWC An important part of writing about science is the 'quality of your written communication'. In exams, you can lose marks in some questions if you have spelled words incorrectly or not used the right format for your answer. This icon shows you where writing skills are being looked at and explained.

Easy cross-references show links to other related skills.

Activities

The activities section presents some interesting and relevant scientific stories to look at. It will also allow you to use your skills, by answering the questions.

Questions test a range of essential skills including How Science Works, Maths Skills and Quality of Written Communication. Easy cross-references let you look up explanations of the skills needed to answer questions you are struggling with.

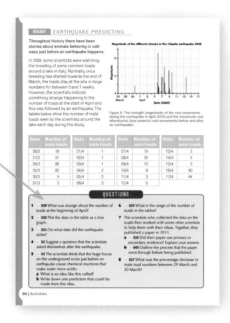

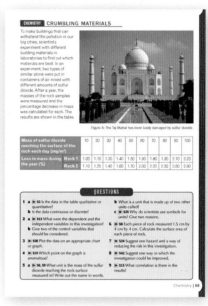

Answers

There are answers to all the questions in the book so that you can easily check your progress.

Many of the answers have tips *in italics* on how you could improve or warnings about mistakes that often get made. They are worth reading carefully.

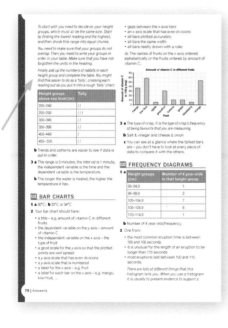

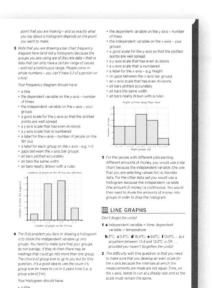

The **scientific method** is a process (series of steps) that scientists use to show whether their ideas are correct or not. A man called Ibn al Haytham, who was born just over a thousand years ago in what is now Iraq, laid the foundations of this method. He is often called 'the first scientist' because he was the first to use scientific experiments to test ideas.

Figure A: Ibn al Haytham (965–1039).

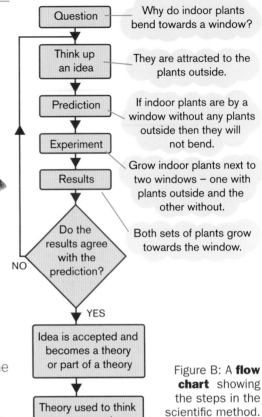

Figure B: A **flow chart** showing the steps in the scientific method.

In the scientific method you think up an idea that answers a question. You then use your idea to make a **prediction** (saying what you think will happen in an experiment).

You then compare what happens in your experiment (the results) with your prediction. If they match then it is likely that your idea is correct. Your idea may become a **theory** (an explanation about why things happen, which *many* experiments have shown to be correct).

QUESTIONS

Level Booster

★★★ explain why some results support or do not support a prediction

★★ recognise if results agree with a prediction or not

★ recognise that results need to be compared with predictions

1 a ★ What is a prediction?
   b ★ Why are results compared with predictions in the scientific method?
2 a ★★ Do the results in the example shown in Figure B agree with the prediction?
   b ★★★ What does this tell you about the idea? Explain your reasoning.
3 ★★★ In the 17th century, people thought that meat produced maggots. In 1668, Francesco Redi (1626–1697) thought that flies laying eggs on the meat caused the maggots.

He did experiments to test this, including the one shown in Figure C. Redraw the flow chart in Figure B to show Redi's experiment.

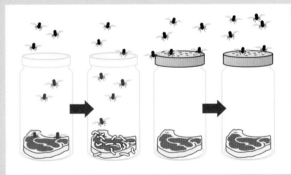

Figure C: One of Redi's experiments.

Links

Learn about scientific questions ⏩ **S2**
Learn about hypotheses and predictions ⏩ **S3**
Learn about theories ⏩ **S4**

The difference between scientific questions and other questions is that scientific ones can be answered by doing experiments (in which something is observed or measured).

Questions such as: 'Why do plants grow towards light?' or 'How do rainbows form?' are scientific. Not all scientific questions have answers at the moment because we don't have enough information from experiments to answer them. This may be because not enough experiments have been done or because the experiments are too expensive or are impossible to do with current technology.

Questions that involve personal choices are not scientific. For example, 'Should I go to the party?' and 'Why is blue the best colour?' are not scientific questions because you can't do experiments to answer them.

Experiments to answer scientific questions can be of different types (e.g. fair tests (S13), surveys, experiments with control groups (S14). Sometimes, it's easier to 'look something up' and get information from other people's experiments.

Figure A: Scientific questions are answered by doing experiments.

Figure B: Not all questions are scientific.

QUESTIONS

Level Booster

★★★ identify the features of scientific and non-scientific questions

★★ recognise that science has not yet answered all scientific questions

★ recognise scientific and non-scientific questions

1 a ★ Look at Figure B. Which question is non-scientific?

  b ★★★ Explain your choice.

2 ★★ Suggest why the following questions have no answers – explain your reasoning.

  a All cells contain a genetic code. Scientists are steadily working out the codes for all living things. So, what is the genetic code for a giraffe?

  b Is there liquid water under the surface of Callisto (one of Jupiter's moons)?

3 a ★ Which of these questions are scientific: Which is more fizzy, Pepsi or Coke? Why is cricket so boring? What gives wine gums their taste? Why do skis slide on snow? Why is Newcastle United the best football team in the world, ever? Why do offices have white walls?

  b ★★★ Suggest two features of all scientific questions. Looking at **S1** may help you.

Links

Learn about how scientific questions are answered ▶▶ **S1**

Learn about hypotheses and predictions ▶▶ **S3**

Learn about fair tests ▶▶ **S13**

Learn about control groups ▶▶ **S14**

After a scientific question has been asked, a scientist thinks up an idea that explains how or why something happens. This idea is called a **hypothesis**.

Scientists think creatively. They invent new connections between things that are already known, to form hypotheses. They then test them, using experiments, the results of which might cause the hypothesis to be changed.

Fiction authors work in a similar way. They have characters and locations that they put together in different ways as a book goes on. Editors then test the book!

QWC The term 'depends on' provides a useful writing frame for writing down ideas (see Figure C). Scientists use their ideas to make **predictions** that can be tested in experiments. You can use the words 'if … then …' as a writing frame for making predictions.

Scientists give reasons for thinking that their ideas and predictions are correct before doing experiments. Many experiments are expensive to do and organisations that give money to scientists want to be sure that the experiments will be successful.

Figure A: Anne Rooney is a fiction author.

Figure B: Theodor Schwann thought creatively to develop our understanding of cells.

A scientific question is one that can be answered by doing an experiment. *Why is the water in a tap hotter at 07:00 than it is at 06:30?*

Question

The temperature of some water **depends on** the length of time it is heated for.

Think up an idea (hypothesis)

Try to explain why you think your idea and/or your prediction is correct. *…because with a longer time more heat energy is transferred to the water.*

Think about using 'if … then …' If $20 \, cm^3$ of water is heated for a longer time **then** it will reach a higher temperature than if it is heated for a shorter time.

Prediction

Experiment

Figure C: Answering a scientific question.

QUESTIONS

Level Booster

★★★ describe how creative thinking is used in scientific developments

★★ describe how existing knowledge is used when thinking up hypotheses

★ use scientific ideas to write predictions

1 QWC ★ Theodor Schwann (1810–1882) used a microscope to test his idea that all cells have nuclei. Write a prediction that Schwann might have made, using his idea.

2 QWC ★ The growth of a plant depends on the amount of fertiliser in the soil. Is this a hypothesis or a prediction? Explain your reasoning.

3 QWC Write predictions for these ideas:
   a ★ Chocolate causes spots.
   b ★ The temperature at which water boils depends on the amount of salt added.

4 ★★★ Suggest an observation or a piece of information used to develop the hypothesis in Figure C.

5 a ★★★ Why is answering scientific questions a creative process?
   b ★★★ How is a fiction plot judged differently to a hypothesis?

Links

Learn about the scientific method ▶▶ S1
Learn about theories ▶▶ S4

The results from experiments are used as **evidence** to say if a scientific idea (**hypothesis**) is right or wrong. If the results agree with the predictions, we say that the 'evidence *supports* the hypothesis'.

An idea that has been tested and been shown to be correct (or not to be wrong) becomes a **theory**. So a theory is a hypothesis with evidence to support it.

A theory may contain many hypotheses, all with supporting evidence. These hypotheses come from different scientists building on each other's work. The **kinetic theory** is built on the work of hundreds of scientists. Its many hypotheses deal with how solids, liquids and gases behave when they are heated, squashed, hit, etc.

A theory:
* allows predictions to be made
* explains all the observations
* may explain other observations that weren't thought to be linked to the theory
* can be tested.

"I've narrowed it to two hypotheses: it grew or we shrank."

Figure A

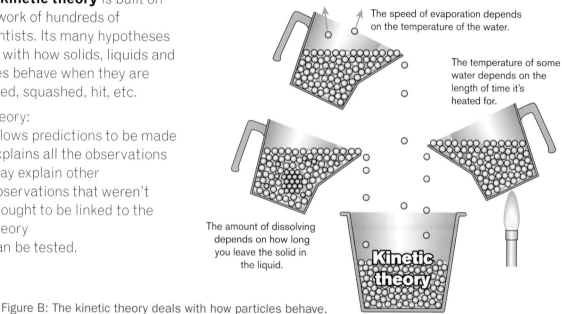

The speed of evaporation depends on the temperature of the water.

The temperature of some water depends on the length of time it's heated for.

The amount of dissolving depends on how long you leave the solid in the liquid.

Kinetic theory

Figure B: The kinetic theory deals with how particles behave.

QUESTIONS

1 a ★ Why do scientists do experiments? Use the word 'evidence' in your answer.

b ★ What does 'the evidence supports the idea' mean?

2 ★★ Preet says 'I have a theory that the netball team did not play very well because Thursdays are unlucky.' What is scientifically wrong with her statement?

3 ★★ Robert Boyle (1627–1691) found that some air had the same mass after being squashed. Daniel Bernoulli (1700–1782) found that squashed air springs back to its original volume. They didn't live at the same time, so why are their evidence and ideas found in the same theory?

4 ★★★ Choose one hypothesis from Figure B and explain how a scientist would test it.

Links
Learn about theories and the scientific method ▶▶ **S1**
Learn about data ▶▶ **S5**

Data is the term for numbers or words that can be organised to give information. Data given as numbers comes with something telling you what the number means (e.g. a unit of measurement, percentage). Numbers that come with meanings are **values**. '5cm' is a value but '5' is not (you don't know what the '5' refers to).

Data as numbers is **quantitative data**. Quantitative data can be:

✳ **continuous** – each value can be any number between two limits

✳ **discrete** – each value can only be one of a limited choice of numbers.

Data that is not in the form of numbers is **qualitative** or **categoric data** (data put into categories).

Data must be organised to make it easier to understand. It is then used as **evidence** to show that an idea might be right or wrong. A simple way of organising data is to put it in order (e.g. number order, alphabetical order).

Data for this horse

Qualitative (categoric)
brown body
friendly

Quantitative

discrete
4 legs
2 eyes

continuous
1.52 m tall
mass of 453.59 kg

Figure A: Different types of data. Don't get confused – numbers come in 'quantities' and so are quantitative.

Figure B: In court, data about someone is organised into evidence and is then presented.

QUESTIONS

Level Booster

★★★ plan to collect and organise different types of data from investigations

★★ order data in the best ways to be used as evidence

★ identify qualitative and quantitative data

1 ★ What types of data are:
   a favourite colours
   b shoe sizes
   c heights in metres?

2 ★ Which of the following are values?
   25 mm, green, 60%, 0.089 cm³, 2012, chicken, metres

3 **a** ★ What types of data does this list contain?
   Team B – 5 points, Team C – 7 points, Team A – 2 points, Team D – 3 points
   b ★★ Order this data in three different ways.

4 ★★★ In an investigation, different masses of magnesium were added to hydrochloric acid and data was collected about how warm the tube became. Describe the types of data that could be collected.

Links

Learn about presenting data ▶▶ **S30, S31, S32, S33, S34, S36, S37**
Learn about units ▶▶ **S6**

It is useful if everyone uses the same measurement system. All scientists use the **SI system** (Système International). The units used in this system, for five basic quantities, are shown in the table.

Quantity	Unit name	Symbol
length	metre	m
mass	gram	g
time	second	s
temperature	degree Celsius	°C
current	ampere, amp	A

Additions are put onto the units to make them bigger or smaller. Be very careful about writing capital and lower case letters (they mean different things).

Name addition	Symbol addition	Meaning (words)	Meaning (numbers)
micro-	μ	one millionth	0.000 001
milli-	m	one thousandth	0.001
centi-	c	one hundredth	0.01
deci-	d	one tenth	0.1
kilo-	k	× one thousand	1000
mega-	M	× one million	1 000 000

Other units are formed from the basic units in the first table above. Here are some examples.

Quantity	Example units
energy	J (joule)
voltage	V (volt)
pressure	Pa (pascal)
power	W (watt)
frequency	Hz (hertz)
force	N (newton)

QUESTIONS

Level Booster

★★★ use the correct SI units in a wide range of situations

★★ recognise the importance of the SI system

★ recognise, write down and interconvert simple SI units

1 ★ What do the following symbols mean?
   a m; **b** °C; **c** kg; **d** mm; **e** μg; **f** kHz; **g** MW; **h** mV; **i** dm; **j** cs

2 ★ How many millimetres are there in the following?
   a 1 cm; **b** 10 m; **c** 10 mm; **d** 100 μm

3 ★★ Why did all scientists around the world agree to use the SI system?

4 ★★★ Which SI units would you most often use to measure the following?
   a The distance covered by a car on a motorway in one hour.
   b The mass of a single human hair.
   c The shortest amount of time for which a camera shutter can stay open.
   d The voltage in the wires coming from a power station.

Links

Learn about units using indices ▶▶ **S7**
Learn about compound measures ▶▶ **S9**

Some SI units are formed by multiplying the same unit a number of times. The diagram shows how this works for **areas** and **volumes**. You show the number of times a unit has been multiplied together using a **power** or **index**. This is a little number written after and above the unit symbol (e.g. m^2).

Quantity	Example units	Example names
area	mm^2, cm^2, m^2	millimetres squared or square millimetres
volume	cm^3, dm^3, m^3	decimetres cubed or cubic decimetres

Converting between large and small units in the SI system is easy because you always use multiples of 10. For example, to convert 5.5 km into mm, you would start by saying that 1 km is 1000 m, and so 5.5 km is $5.5 \times 1000 = 5500$ m. Then 1 m is 1000 mm, so 5500 m is $5500 \times 1000 = 5\,500\,000$ mm.

When converting between units in **index form** you need to remember to multiply the number by the unit's index power. For example, 1 m contains 100 cm but in 1 m^3 there $100\,cm \times 100\,cm \times 100\,cm = 1\,000\,000\,cm^3$.

Numbers can also have indices. For example, 5^2 means 5 multiplied by itself (or 5×5) – this is 'five squared'. 5^3 means $5 \times 5 \times 5$, which is 'five cubed'.

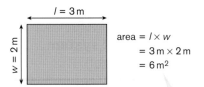

$l = 3\,m$

$w = 2\,m$

area $= l \times w$
$= 3\,m \times 2\,m$
$= 6\,m^2$

We've multiplied metres by itself (two 'lots' of metres), and so the unit is m^2. We say this as 'metres squared' or 'square metres' (which just means metres multiplied by metres). The little 'two' is the index.

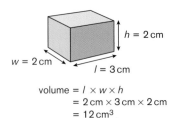

$h = 2\,cm$

$w = 2\,cm$

$l = 3\,cm$

volume $= l \times w \times h$
$= 2\,cm \times 3\,cm \times 2\,cm$
$= 12\,cm^3$

We've multiplied centimetres by itself twice, and so the unit is cm^3 (three 'lots' of centimetres). We say this as 'centimetres cubed or 'cubic centimetres'.

Figure A: Using **index form** saves time and is recognised by all scientists.

QUESTIONS

Level Booster

- ★★★ interconvert SI units involving index notation
- ★★ recognise the importance of and use index notation for numbers and symbols
- ★ recognise the squares of numbers

1 ★ How would you *say* the following?
a m^3; **b** km^2; **c** 5^2; **d** 8^2; **e** 9^3

2 ★★ Give two reasons why index form is used in science.

3 a ★★ A box has sides 10 cm by 5 cm by 6 cm. What is its volume?
b What are the areas of each of its six sides?

4 ★★★ A rectangular field is 1 km long and 55 m wide. What is its area in m^2?

5 ★★★ A square swimming pool of width 5 m is 2 m deep. What is its volume in dm^3?

Links

Learn about SI units ▶▶ **S6**
Learn about calculating perimeters, areas and volumes ▶▶ **S8**

S8 CALCULATING PERIMETERS, AREAS AND VOLUMES

The diagram shows how to calculate the **perimeters**, **areas** and **volumes** of different shapes. Shapes that involve circles use a number called **pi** (written as π). This number never changes and is approximately 3.14.

The perimeter of a circle is called the **circumference**. The **diameter** is the length of a straight line that passes through the centre of the circle and meets the circumference at two points. The **radius** of the circle is the distance between the centre and the circumference.

If you need area or volume measurements in an investigation, you must decide what **data** to collect and what calculations you will use to turn that data into **evidence**. You need to choose the right equipment to make your measurements.

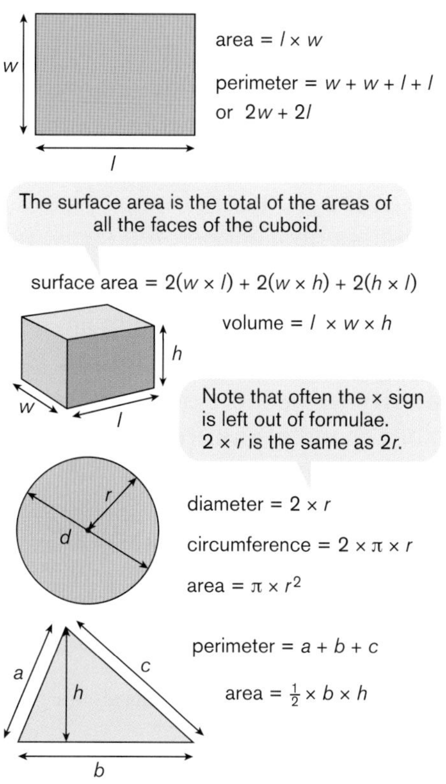

area = $l \times w$

perimeter = $w + w + l + l$
or $2w + 2l$

The surface area is the total of the areas of all the faces of the cuboid.

surface area = $2(w \times l) + 2(w \times h) + 2(h \times l)$

volume = $l \times w \times h$

Note that often the $\times$ sign is left out of formulae. $2 \times r$ is the same as $2r$.

diameter = $2 \times r$

circumference = $2 \times \pi \times r$

area = $\pi \times r^2$

perimeter = $a + b + c$

area = $\frac{1}{2} \times b \times h$

Figure A: Calculating perimeters, areas and volumes.

QUESTIONS

Level Booster

★★★ plan measurements and calculate the perimeter and area of circles

★★ plan measurements and calculate the area of a triangle and the volume of a cuboid

★ plan measurements and calculate the perimeters and areas of rectangular shapes

1 ★ A playing field is 100 m by 75 m.
  a Which of the following would you use to measure these distances?
  30 cm ruler, roll of string, stop watch, measuring tape
  b What is the perimeter of the field? Show your working.
  c What is the area of the field? Show your working.

2 ★ A quadrat is a square frame used in biology. One quadrat has sides of 0.5 m. What is its area?

3 A heating block measures 4 cm by 6 cm by 10 cm.
  a ★ What is its surface area?
  b ★★ What is its volume?

4 A cube has 1 cm sides and a cuboid measures 2 cm by 0.2 cm by 1.5 cm.
  a ★ Which has the greater surface area?
  b ★★ Which has the bigger volume?

5 ★★ A triangular patch of ground has sides 1.5 m, 2 m and 4 m.
  a What is the patch's perimeter?
  b What other measurement would you make to calculate the patch's area?

6 ★★★ A Petri dish is 9 cm in diameter.
  a What is its circumference?
  b What is the area of its top surface?

Links

Learn about SI units ▶▶ **S6**
Learn about index form ▶▶ **S7**
Learn about ratios ▶▶ **S27**

Sometimes you need two units to describe a **value**. For example, a unit for speed must tell us 'the distance travelled in a certain amount of time'. So a unit for speed has a unit for distance *and* a unit for time. If the distance is in metres and the time is in seconds, the unit tells us the 'number of metres travelled in one second' or 'metres per second'. You show 'per' as a slash '/' and so write the unit as m/s.

Units made up of other units are called **compound units** or **compound measures**. We also use them for **density** (a measure of how tightly packed things are in a space) and **pressure** (a measure of the force on a certain area).

Distance in metres… …and time in seconds

…so speed in metres/second (m/s)

Figure A: Using compound units for speed.

At its fastest, the truck can travel 42 km in 1 hour – a top speed of 42 km/h.

If force is in newtons (N) and area is in square metres (m^2), the pressure is in newtons per square metre (N/m^2). When empty, this truck has a weight of about 6 MN. Each of the six tyres supports one sixth of this weight (1 MN). Each tyre has an area of 2 m^2 in contact with the ground.

Each cubic metre (m^3) of steel has a mass of about 7800 kg. Steel has a density of about 7800 kg/m^3 (or 7.8 g/cm^3).

1.5 g of rubber has a volume of 1 cm^3 (1 cubic centimetre). Rubber has a density of 1.5 g/cm^3.

Figure B: Some compound units.

QUESTIONS

Level Booster

★★★ combine units into compound units

★★ interpret compound units

★ recognise some units for speed

1 ★ Which of these are *not* units for speed? km/h, N/cm^2, cm/s, m/h, m/g, mm/°C, m/s

2 **a** ★★ Which of these are *not* compound units?
   km, N/cm^2, cm/s, °C, kg/m^3, m, V/m, g

   b ★★ For each of the *compound* units listed in part **a**, write out its name in full.

3 ★★★ If distance is in metres and time is in seconds, what is the unit for speed?

4 ★★★ If time is in days and distance is in centimetres, what is the unit for speed?

5 ★★★ 1 cm^3 of magnesium has a mass of 1.7 g. What is its density?

6 ★★★ Look at Figure B. Which has the greater density, steel or rubber? Explain your reasoning.

7 ★★★ What is the pressure under one tyre of the truck in Figure B?

8 ★★★ The rate at which energy is converted is the number of joules of energy that are converted in each second. What unit would be used?

Links

Learn about SI units ▶▶ **S6**

Learn about index form ▶▶ **S7**

S10 MANAGING LARGE NUMBERS

Numbers are easier to understand when written in digits and not words. For example:

two billion four million three thousand one hundred and sixty-two is easier to understand when written as 2004003162.

We can make large numbers even clearer by putting the digits into groups of three – 2004003162 becomes 2 004 003 162

Some people use commas instead of gaps but this can be confusing because in some countries they use commas (,) to mean decimal points (.)!

Using groups of three digits makes it much easier to see where the place values are (e.g. where the thousands place is in the number).

EXTENSION **Standard form** is a way of writing numbers using index form (S7) (which can make calculations with large numbers easier). To write a number in standard form you shift the decimal point to the left until there is a single digit (1 to 9) in the units place. You then write the number of places the decimal point has been shifted as a power of 10 – that's a '10' with an index.

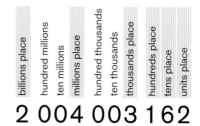

Figure A: Putting digits into groups of three makes it easier to see the place values.

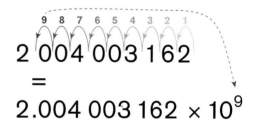

Figure B: Using standard form.

QUESTIONS

Level Booster

★★★ interpret numbers in standard form
★★ recognise powers of 10
★ recognise place values in big numbers

1 a ★ What is the hundreds digit in 2 078 517 829?
   b What is the thousands digit in 8 003 593?
   c What is the millions digit in 56 067 868 465?

2 ★ Write out these numbers in words:
   a 98624; **b** 6845709

3 ★ Write out the numbers in question 2 in a clearer form.

4 ★★ In the number 3×10^7, what does the little '7' mean?

5 ★★★ Write out these numbers in full:
   a 2×10^6; **b** 8.65×10^4; **c** 1.089678×10^5

Links

Learn about SI units ▶▶ **S6**
Learn about index form ▶▶ **S7**

S11 ESTIMATES: ROUNDING AND SAMPLES

Scientists often **estimate** numbers. This means using a rough calculation to come up with a value that is approximately correct.

Estimating:
* saves time
* helps you to focus on the important parts of what you are doing.

One way of estimating is to round figures up or down. Figure A shows how this is done. You just need to be careful about which place value you choose. If you make an estimate too approximate then you may not be able to use it to work out an answer.

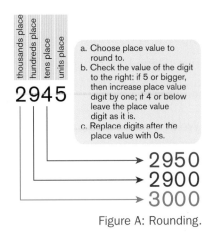

a. Choose place value to round to.
b. Check the value of the digit to the right: if 5 or bigger, then increase place value digit by one; if 4 or below leave the place value digit as it is.
c. Replace digits after the place value with 0s.

Figure A: Rounding.

You can also use part of some data (a **sample**) to estimate other values outside the sample. For example, to work out the number of spots in Figure B, you count the spots in a small sample area. You then calculate how many times bigger the whole area is compared with the sample area. Multiplying this number by the number of spots counted gives an estimate of the total number of spots in the whole drawing.

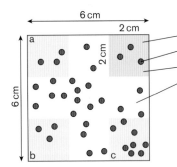

1 Choose a sample area.
2 Count spots in sample area (= 3).
3 Work out size of sample area. Area = length × width (= 2 × 2 = 4 cm²).
4 Work out size of whole area (= 6 × 6 = 36 cm²).
5 Calculate how many times bigger whole area is compared with sample (= 36 ÷ 4 = 9).
6 The number of spots in the whole area will be about 9 times more (= 9 × 3 = 27).
7 We estimate that there are about 27 spots in the whole area.

Figure B: Estimating data from a sample.

QUESTIONS

Level Booster

★★★ make the estimates best suited to solving a problem quickly
★★ use a sample to estimate numbers outside the sample
★ make estimates by rounding numbers

1 ★ Round the following numbers to the nearest: **a** ten; **b** hundred; **c** thousand.
   i 5689; **ii** 2438; **iii** 7555; **iv** 56069;
   v 235689

2 ★★ Round 3789067 to the nearest ten thousand.

3 ★★ Use the pale yellow squares (**a**, **b** and **c**) on Figure B to calculate three estimates of the total number of spots in the drawing. Show all your working.
   d ★★★ Suggest how you could get a better estimate for the number of dots.

4 ★★★ Aroon wants to know if all the sports pitches in a park are the same length. He rounds all his measurements to tens of metres. What is the problem with this?

Links

Learn about samples and bias ▶▶ **S12**
Learn about significant figures ▶▶ **S18**
Learn about means ▶▶ **S20**
Learn about estimating from graphs ▶▶ **S33, S34**

Bias is when evidence is all moved in one direction. This can make you believe something that is not really true.

Bias can be caused:
* by mistake – e.g. problems with experiments
* on purpose – when someone wants you to believe something.

When you use samples to make estimates, it is quite easy to be biased. Look at Figure B. If you estimate the number of spots in the whole drawing using square A3, it comes out to 27 spots. If you use square A2, the estimate is 18 spots and with square C3 it is 72. The actual number is 38.

If you take too few samples you don't get good estimates, but if you take too many samples it takes too long. So for Figure B you might decide to estimate using three or four smaller sample squares.

Taking samples from just one place can also cause bias – so you need to choose samples at **random**. Here you could put the names of each square into a hat and draw out three names. Other ways of making random choices include throwing dice.

Although the gun was aimed at the centre of the target, the bullets all ended up in the upper left of the target. There is bias. This might be due to the gun or to the person who is firing it.

Figure A: A way of thinking about bias.

This is square A3 (row A, column 3).

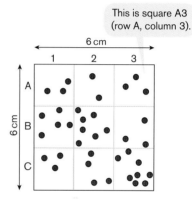

Figure B: Small sample sizes can cause bias.

QUESTIONS

Level Booster

★★★ avoid bias when using samples
★★ explain the causes and effects of bias
★ describe what bias is

1 a ★ Look at Figure A. Are the shots biased up or down?
  b ★ Are the shots biased left or right?
  c ★ Suggest a cause of this bias.

2 ★★ Matilda's estimate for the number of spots in Figure B is 18. Suggest how her estimate came to be so poor.

3 a ★★ Mark only talks about the good points of his football team. Why?
  b Why is this an example of bias?

4 ★★★ Asha is estimating the number of mushrooms growing in a field. Suggest how she can avoid bias.

Links

Learn about bias that's on purpose ▶▶ **S43**
Learn about accuracy and precision ▶▶ **S16**

A **variable** is something that can change. It is sometimes called a **factor**.

In an investigation, you select values for one variable and measure what happens to another. The variable that you change is the **independent variable.** The variable that you measure is the **dependent variable**. The dependent variable *depends on* the independent variable.

A **control variable** or **fixed variable** is another factor that can affect the dependent variable. You have to try to stop any control variables changing. When planning an investigation you list all the control variables and decide how to stop them changing.

In a **fair test** the only thing that changes the dependent variable is the independent variable. You need to:

* identify the independent variable
* identify the dependent variable
* stop the control variables changing.

Figure A: Anything that can vary (change) is a variable. Shoes can vary in shape, materials, colour, etc.

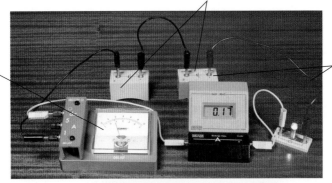

independent variable: the number of cells

dependent variable: the current

control variables:
i) same type of cell used
ii) rest of circuit kept the same

Figure B: A fair test used to answer the question: Does the current increase, the more cells you have?

QUESTIONS

Level Booster

★★★ explain how different variables affect one another

★★ select the appropriate variables for an investigation

★ identify different variables in an investigation

1 ★ John dissolves different amounts of salt in several 100 cm³ samples of water. He finds the boiling point of each solution, using the same heating apparatus and thermometer. Identify the different variables.

2 Here are some scientific questions:
  i Does the amount of light affect the number of blowfly maggots found in an area?
  ii Are some antacids better than others at neutralising acids?
  iii Do bigger magnets pick up more paper clips than small ones do?
  a ★★For each investigation select the independent, dependent and control variables.
  b ★★★ Explain how one control variable in each investigation could cause problems.

Links
Learn about controls ▶▶ **S14**
Learn about correlations ▶▶ **S15**

A fair test is not possible if there are too many **control variables**.

A **control experiment** is the same as a fair test, but you include a **control** or a **control group**. The control uses exactly the same set-up as the main part of the experiment, but without the independent variable.

Controls are used when investigating living things because organisms vary so much. The organisms are divided into groups, making sure that the groups are as similar to each other as possible. The independent variable is

Figure A: Huge numbers of control variables (e.g. sex, age, ethnic background, weight, height in humans) mean that you can't use fair tests.

changed for each group, but one group is a control. The results from the control make it easier to see if changes are due to the independent variable only.

Group A: 1 dose of drug X   Group B: 2 doses of drug X   Group C: 3 doses of drug X   Control: no drug X

Figure B: Controls are used in drug tests. The control shows whether it is the drug having an effect, or something else.

QUESTIONS

Level Booster

★★★ give reasons for using or not using a control experiment

★★ explain what a control experiment is

★ recognise investigations that cannot be done using a fair test

1 ★ Which of the following investigations could not use a fair test?
  A The current in a circuit when the number of bulbs is changed.
  B The effect of an antacid on an acid.
  C The effect of an antacid on reducing the effects of heartburn in someone.
  D The effect on Arctic foxes of increasing the average temperature.

2 ★★ How is a control experiment different from a fair test?

3 **a** ★★ Look at the experiment on page 18, in **S13**. Suggest a control.
  b ★★★ Would you *not* use a control experiment in this case? Explain your reasoning.

4 ★★★ A drug company wants to find out if its new drug for headaches is better than the standard drugs. Explain how the trial would be carried out.

Links

Learn about samples and bias ▶▶ **S12**
Learn about variables and fair tests ▶▶ **S13**

A **relationship** (or **correlation**) is a link between variables. If one variable changes, so does another.

In experiments you test how an **independent variable** affects a **dependent variable**. You look at your results to see if there is a link between the changes in the two variables. If a steady change in one is matched by a steady change in the other then there is a relationship.

It can be difficult to see patterns in data, so a better way of spotting relationships is to use **scatter graphs**. These also show whether a relationship is strong or weak. The closer all the results stick to a pattern, the stronger the relationship.

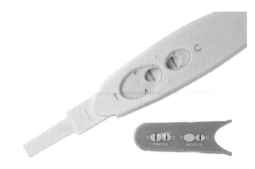

Figure A: There is a simple relationship between a woman being pregnant and a chemical called hCG being present in her urine. Pregnancy test kits detect this chemical.

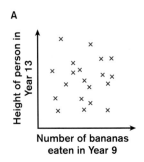 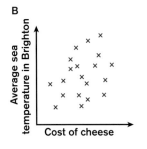 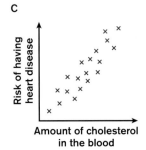 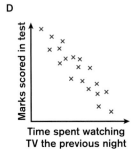

A — Height of person in Year 13 / Number of bananas eaten in Year 9

B — Average sea temperature in Brighton / Cost of cheese

C — Risk of having heart disease / Amount of cholesterol in the blood

D — Marks scored in test / Time spent watching TV the previous night

The stronger a relationship, the more likely it is that changes in one variable have actually caused changes in the other. However, a relationship between two variables does not necessarily mean that one has caused the other.

Figure B: Scatter graphs are useful for showing correlation.

QUESTIONS

Level Booster

★★★ justify a choice of how to present data

★★ identify relationships as being strong or weak

★ spot relationships in results

1 ★ Look at Figure A. What is the relationship?

2 ★ A race is won by a Year 8 boy. A Year 6 boy finishes 3rd, a Year 4 boy finishes 4th and a Year 7 boy finishes 2nd. What is the relationship?

3 In Figure B, in which graph or graphs is there:
a ★ no relationship
b ★★ a strong relationship
c ★★ a weak relationship?

4 ★★ Look at Figure B. Why does graph C suggest that changes in the independent variable do actually cause changes in the dependent variable?

5 ★★★ Why do scientists use scatter graphs to show their results?

Links

Learn about variables and fair tests ▶▶ **S13**
Learn about scatter graphs and lines of best fit ▶▶ **S34**

Words that we use in everyday English often have different meanings in science.

We often use the words 'accurate' and 'precise' to mean the same thing. In science they mean different things.

- **Accuracy** is how close a measurement is to the true value. You need to use apparatus that gives results accurate enough to draw a conclusion. For example, to measure the height of a person you could use a metre rule, accurate to 1 cm. To measure the distance a car travels in an hour you don't need this amount of accuracy.

- **Precision** is how well a set of the same measurements are grouped together. If they are all close together, the measurements are described as being precise. The more precise results are, the more certain you can be that they are correct.

Figure A: You must be careful about some words in science. 'Mass' and 'weight' are not the same in science.

shots are:
- not accurate
- not precise

shots are:
- accurate
- not precise

shots are:
- not accurate
- precise

shots are:
- accurate
- precise

Figure B: Accuracy and precision are different.

QUESTIONS

Level Booster

★★★ justify investigation planning in terms of accuracy and precision

★★ explain what precision is and why it is important

★ explain what accuracy is and why it is important

1 The tables show readings taken by Liz and the real values of those readings.

Liz's reading	Real value
15.9 cm	16.0 cm
15.7 cm	16.0 cm
15.8 cm	16.0 cm
15.8 cm	16.0 cm

Liz's reading	Real value
16.7 cm	17.1 cm
16.4 cm	17.1 cm
16.2 cm	17.1 cm
17.0 cm	17.1 cm

a ★ Which is Liz's most accurate reading in each set? Explain your reasoning.

b ★ Which was Liz's least accurate reading?

2 ★ Suggest a problem with having inaccurate readings.

3 a ★★ Look at the table in question 1. For which set of readings are Liz's readings more precise? Explain your reasoning.

b ★★ Why are precise readings more useful than readings that are not so precise?

4 ★★★ In question **1**, Liz made her measurements while investigating this question: Which of two species of bean plant grows taller? Are her results accurate and precise enough to draw a conclusion? Explain your reasoning.

Links

Learn about bias ▶▶ **S12**

Learn about errors in measurement ▶▶ **S17**

Learn about repeatability and reliability ▶▶ **S22**

There will always be differences between measurements of the same thing. This is called 'error'. The more errors in a set of results, the less sure you can be that they are correct. Sometimes errors cause measurements to be spread widely. At other times errors cause all your measurements to be shifted away from the true value by the same amount.

Human error is when people make mistakes. Common human errors occur when people don't read scales correctly. When you read a scale you should be level with it.

Human error can also happen even if measuring is done correctly. For example, a poorly planned investigation may not give any useful results.

Apparatus can also cause errors. For example, when using a balance you need to set it to zero before measuring a mass. If measuring apparatus is not set up properly, you won't get correct readings.

Look from too high, and your reading will be too high.

correct reading

Look from too low, and your reading will be too low.

The surfaces of some liquids curve in a measuring cylinder. It's only the very outside of the surface that curves and so the reading is taken from the lowest point of the surface. To do this, you need to be level with the surface of the liquid.

Figure A: How to read the level of liquid in a measuring cylinder.

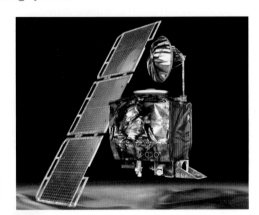

Figure B: Poor planning meant that this £210 million spacecraft *Mars Climate Orbiter* fell apart. A computer programmer used the wrong units of measurement in part of the software.

QUESTIONS

Level Booster

★★★ look for errors in results, explaining causes and improvements to planning

★★ describe how common errors can occur

★ describe how errors can affect the usefulness of results

1 ★ What is 'human error'?

2 Here are two sets of results for the same experiment.

Group	Mass of copper oxide (g) needed to neutralise 10 cm³ of acid		
A	8.3	8.5	8.2
B	7.9	8.5	6.3

a ★ Which set of results contains more errors? How can you tell?

b ★ Why is it a problem if a set of results contains many errors?

c ★★ Suggest two ways in which errors could have occurred in this experiment.

3 The measuring cylinder in Figure A has a scale marked in cm³.

a ★★ What is the correct reading for the amount of water in the cylinder?

b ★★ How should you read a scale to get a correct reading?

c ★★ What reading would be got by looking at the scale from too high?

4 ★★★ Look at the table opposite. Explain how better results could be obtained.

Links

Learn about significant figures ▶▶ **S18**
Learn about anomalous results ▶▶ **S19**

S18 SIGNIFICANT FIGURES

Significant figures are the digits that show a value's accuracy. For example, a town's population is 10675. To two significant figures this is 11 000 (only *two* figures now show the value, the rest are zeros). 11 000 is a less accurate value than 10675.

Less accurate measuring devices produce values with fewer significant figures, compared with more accurate devices.

We often use fewer significant figures because:
* they make calculations easier
* less accurate measuring apparatus is cheaper
* less accurate measuring apparatus is quicker to use
* you often don't need very accurate values to come to a conclusion.

When doing calculations, do not give your answer to more significant figures than the least accurate value that you started with.

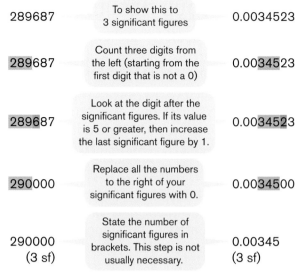

289687	To show this to 3 significant figures	0.0034523
289687	Count three digits from the left (starting from the first digit that is not a 0)	0.0034523
289687	Look at the digit after the significant figures. If its value is 5 or greater, then increase the last significant figure by 1.	0.0034523
290000	Replace all the numbers to the right of your significant figures with 0.	0.0034500
290000 (3 sf)	State the number of significant figures in brackets. This step is not usually necessary.	0.00345 (3 sf)

Figure A: Changing significant figures.

Matilda has a mass of 65 kg. She loses one hair. What is her new mass?

mass = 0.2 g

mass = 65 000 g   mass = 64 999.8 g

This figure makes no sense because 65 000 g was only correct to two significant figures. We don't know Matilda's mass to enough accuracy to subtract the mass of the hair. Matilda's real mass could be anywhere between 64 500 and 65 499 g! So Matilda's mass is still 65 000 g (or 65 kg).

Figure B: Be careful with the number of significant figures.

QUESTIONS

1 ★ The populations of some towns are: 70 000, 62 796 and 59 700.
   a Which value is the most accurate?
   b Which is the least accurate?

2 ★ Round the following numbers to the nearest hundred:
   a 5297; **b** 2943; **c** 17 207.

3 ★★ Students are divided into year groups based on their ages in years and months at the start of the school year. Why aren't the ages measured in days?

4 ★★ To measure 1000 cm³ of water, which accuracy of measuring cylinder would you use: scale in 20 cm³ divisions, scale in 1 cm³ divisions or scale in 1 mm³ divisions.

5 ★★ Look at the values in Figure B. How many significant figures does each contain?

6 ★★★ Show both starting numbers in Figure A to:
   a 2 significant figures; **b** 4 significant figures.

7 ★★★ Speed multiplied by time will give the distance travelled. A car drove for 62 seconds at 5.1 m/s. What distance did it travel?

Links
Learn about rounding ▶▶ **S11**
Learn about accuracy ▶▶ **S16**
Learn about means ▶▶ **S20**

An **anomalous result** (or **outlier**) is a measurement that does not fit the pattern of the other results. Anomalous results should be examined to work out how they may have occurred, because of an error. If there are too many anomalous readings in a set of results it can be difficult to draw a conclusion because you can't see the pattern so well.

If you can suggest why one anomalous result in a set of data may be wrong, ignore it when working on your data.

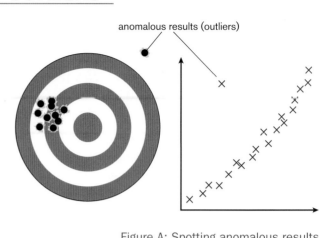

Figure A: Spotting anomalous results.

QUESTIONS

Level Booster

- ★★★ suggest improvements to an investigation to avoid anomalous results
- ★★ deal with anomalous results to avoid them affecting conclusions
- ★ spot readings that do not fit a pattern

1 ★ How can you spot anomalous results in a graph?

2 ★ Look at the graph below. Which result is anomalous? Explain your reasoning.

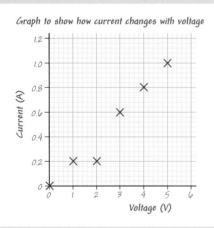

Graph to show how current changes with voltage

Figure B

3 Parni used a stopwatch to time how long a ball bearing took to fall 5 cm through syrup at different temperatures. Her results are shown in the table.

Temp. of golden syrup (°C)	Time taken (s)		
	1st try	2nd try	3rd try
20	39.7	18.9	43.4
34	2.7	3.1	3.3
47	1.2	1.1	1.3
57	0.5	0.6	1.3

a ★ Which results are anomalous? Explain your reasoning.

b ★★ Suggest one way in which one of these outliers could have been caused.

c ★★ What should Parni do to avoid results like these affecting her conclusions?

4 ★★★ An investigation involves counting the number of bubbles produced by some pond weed in 1 minute, in water at different temperatures. Suggest two ways in which anomalous results may be caused and state how you could try to stop them affecting the results.

5 ★★★ An investigation involves adding between 1.1 g and 2 g of solid A to 15 cm³ of liquid B and measuring the temperature increase. Ten different masses are used. Suggest three ways in which anomalous results may be caused and state how you could try to stop them affecting the results.

Links

Learn about means ▶▶ **S20**

S20 MEANS AND RANGES

Repeated measurements usually vary. The **range** of the measurements is the difference between the highest and lowest values. The narrower the range of repeated measurements, the more sure you can be that they are correct.

The true value of a measurement will be inside the range of repeated readings. You can use the readings to **estimate** the value (calculate a value that is roughly correct).

To estimate a true value from a range, you calculate an average called a **mean**:
- add up all your measurements
- divide by the number of measurements you made
- give your answer to the same number of **significant figures** as your original data.

The more measurements used in the calculation, the better the estimate – but the longer it takes. If you have **anomalous results** in your data, and you know how they may have been caused, you can leave them out of the calculation. If you leave them in they may have a big effect on the mean and make it less accurate.

Repeat readings for final temperature (°C)	
Mike's	Jasmin's
27	25.1
28	24.3
38	25.2
23	26.3
22	27.0
	27.1

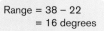
Range = 38 – 22
= 16 degrees

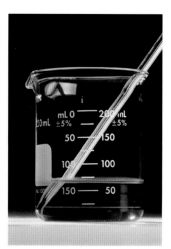

Figure A: Narrow ranges of repeated measurements are better.

How long do I take to zorb down this track?

Test number	Time taken to zorb down the track (s)
1	24.0
2	24.6
3	24.5
4	82.7
5	24.5
6	24.4

There is one outlier – Test 4. We ignore it, otherwise it will give us a poor estimate of the time taken.

Total = 122   Number of tests = 5   Mean = $\frac{122}{5}$ = 24.4 s

Figure B: Calculating a mean.

QUESTIONS

Level Booster

- ★★★ consider the advantages and disadvantages of using means
- ★★ calculate means, consider the quality of data by looking at ranges
- ★ calculate ranges

1 ★ What is the range of the readings in Figure B?

2 a ★ What is the range of Jasmin's results in Figure A?
  b ★★ Calculate the means of Mike's and of Jasmin's results.
  c ★★ Whose results are likely to be more correct? Explain your reasoning.

3 ★★ Anomalous results are often left out of a range. Explain why.

4 a ★ Calculate the mean of *all* the figures in Figure B.
  b ★★★ Use your answer to part a to explain a disadvantage of using means.
  c ★★★ Anomalous results are often left out when calculating means. Suggest a disadvantage of doing this.

Links

Learn about estimates ▶▶ **S11**
Learn about significant figures ▶▶ **S18**
Learn about anomalous data ▶▶ **S19**

Something is **valid** if it does what it's intended to do.

An investigation is valid if the results let you answer the original question. A **fair test** is valid because you measure only the effects of the **independent variable**. You keep the **control variables** the same so they don't affect the **dependent variable**.

Results are valid if the measurements are what was meant to be measured and are **repeatable**. If control variables are not kept the same, the measurements are not valid because the dependent variable is affected by the independent variable *and* other variables.

If the outcome of an investigation is unexpected, you need to check that the method is valid and that the results are valid.

Figure A: A fencer intends to push the foil onto the darker grey part of the opponent's jacket. A hit is only valid if this happens.

control variables (the ones that you keep the same)

are stopped from causing changes

independent variable (the one that you change)

causes changes in ...

dependent variable (the one that you measure)

Figure B: Fair tests are valid.

QUESTIONS

Level Booster

★★★ check the validity of an investigation's method

★★ check the validity of results

★ identify key variables in valid investigations

1 ★ A valid investigation is one to find out how well different materials stop a cup of hot liquid losing heat. Outline the key variables.

2 Osman predicted that the greater the length of a piece of resistance wire in a circuit, the lower the current. His results are shown in the table.

Length of wire (cm)	20	20	20	40	40	40	60	60	60
Current (A)	0.8	0.0	0.1	0.6	0.2	0.9	0.4	0.6	0.8

  a ★ Has Osman measured what he meant to measure? Explain your reasoning.

b ★★ Comment on the validity of his results.

c ★★★ Why must the validity of the method be checked?

3 ★★★ Jordan investigated which kind of milk had the greatest number of bacteria per cm^3. She used a microscope to identify the bacteria and found that raw milk contained 13 different types of bacteria, whole pasteurised milk had 12, semi-skimmed had 11 and UHT had 12. She concluded that raw milk contained the most bacteria. Explain whether this investigation is valid or not.

Links

Learn about fair tests and control variables ▶▶ **S13**
Learn about repeatability and reliability ▶▶ **S22**

S22 REPEATABILITY AND RELIABILITY

The more data you get in an investigation, the more sure you can be of your conclusions.

To check a measurement it is a good idea to repeat it. Measurements that are more or less the same (**precise**) when repeated by a scientist are **repeatable**. If other scientists can repeat the measurements they are said to be **reproducible**.

Good quality data:
- has repeatable measurements (often 3 or 4 repeats for each measurement)
- has many measurements over a **range** that is large enough to see a pattern
- does not have many **anomalous results**
- is reproducible.

Good quality data will allow you to draw a firm conclusion. The word **reliable** is often used to describe data that is of good quality.

Figure A: Using the same bow, both archers had repeatable shots. However, the shots from the same bow were not reproducible by the different archers.

QUESTIONS

Level Booster

★★★ examine the strength of a conclusion based on the quality of the data

★★ describe the features of good quality data

★ explain why measurements should be repeated

1 ★ Why should you repeat readings in investigations where possible?

2 KJ was investigating a pond that is 2 m deep. He took two 10 cm³ samples of pond water – one from a depth of 10 cm and one from a depth of 40 cm. He counted 5 tiny water fleas in the shallow sample, and 16 water fleas in the deeper sample. He concluded that 'the deeper the water, the more water fleas there are'.

a ★ Why is his data not good enough to draw this conclusion?

b ★★ What should KJ do to improve his investigation?

Links
Learn about precision ▶▶ **S16**
Learn about validity ▶▶ **S21**

3 Two groups measured the extension of a spring with different masses hanging on it.

Mass (g)	Extension of spring (cm)			
Group A				
100	4.1	4.1	4.1	4.0
200	7.8	8.0	7.9	8.2
300	12.0	12.1	12.0	11.9
400	16.1	16.1	15.9	16.0
Group B				
100	4.1	4.1	4.1	
200	8.0	8.1	9.1	
300	12.0	11.8	11.9	
400	16.0	15.4	16.1	

a ★★ Which set of data is the more reliable? Explain your reasoning.

b ★★ Look at Group A's results. For which mass are the readings most precise?

c ★★★ Group B concludes that 'if you double the mass, you double the extension of the spring'. Is the data reliable enough to draw this conclusion? Explain your reasoning.

When planning an investigation, it's often difficult to know:

- the **range** of measurements to make (highest and lowest)
- the interval to have between the measurements
- how many measurements to make.

In a **trial run** you carry out an investigation quickly, making a few measurements over a large range. This lets you see a rough pattern, so you can work out the range and the number of measurements you need to be sure of this pattern in the real investigation.

A trial run also means you won't waste time making unnecessary measurements in your investigation (e.g. by having intervals that are too small, which don't allow you to see the overall pattern). It also allows you to make sure that your method works, that you have the correct apparatus (including measuring devices of the right **accuracy**) and that your investigation is safe.

Figure A: In some trial runs, scale models are used to test ideas before a full-sized machine is built to test. This model aeroplane is being tested in a vertical wind tunnel.

QUESTIONS

Level Booster

★★★ justify choices of range and number of readings

★★ use data from a trial run to help planning

★ describe what a trial run is

1 a ★ What is a trial run?
  b ★ State two reasons why you might use a trial run.

Links

Learn about range ▶▶ **S20**
Learn about safety ▶▶ **S24**
Learn about models ▶▶ **S40**

2 Vijay is investigating how the distance travelled by an item propelled by an elastic band, stretched between two nails, depends on its mass. His trial run results are shown in the table:

Mass (g)	10	15	100
Distance travelled (cm)	20	20	2

a ★ State one variable that needs to be kept the same (control variable).

b ★★ Use the trial run results to suggest:
  i a pattern that is occurring
  ii the range of measurements that Vijay should take
  iii the interval between each measurement
  iv the accuracy of the measuring device needed.

c ★★★ Justify the choices you have made in part **b**.

You must plan safe investigations, which means thinking about the **hazards** of the apparatus, chemicals and methods that you want to use. A hazard is when something *can* cause a certain type of harm.

Risk is the *chance* of harm occurring from a hazard. You need to plan to reduce the risks from hazards such as:

✳ broken glass – e.g. reporting it to the teacher to get it cleaned up
✳ chemicals – e.g. not breathing in dust
✳ heating things – e.g. wearing eye protection
✳ using electricity – e.g. switching off a power pack before altering a circuit
✳ spills – e.g. mopping up immediately
✳ living things – e.g. using disinfectants to kill micro-organisms.

explosive   harmful to health   flammable

very toxic (poisonous)   harmful to breathing system   corrosive (attacks skin)

Figure A: Symbols are used to show the hazards of things – especially chemicals.

QUESTIONS

Level Booster

★★★ treat different items in an investigation differently depending on the risk

★★ explain why some ways of controlling risk are better than others

★ recognise risks and the need to control risks

1 a ★ Beth pours 2 cm³ of an alkali into a tube containing some acid. Suggest a hazard in this.
b ★ Suggest a way in which the risk can be reduced.

2 a ★ Mike uses a Bunsen burner to heat water. Suggest two hazards when doing this.
b ★ Suggest a way in which each risk can be reduced.

3 a ★ Look at Figure A. Which symbol might you find on a tank of natural gas (methane)?
b ★ Suggest a way of reducing the risk near the tank.

4 ★★ Sam spills some liquid. Should he put his hand up and call for the teacher or leave his desk and tell the teacher what has happened? Explain your choice.

5 ★★ Apparatus in which bacteria have been grown is heated to high temperature (using an autoclave or burning). Suggest why this is better than spraying the equipment with disinfectant.

6 ★★★ Maddy is taking samples from a stream at 100 m intervals. She holds a small beaker in the stream for each sample. Then she draws up 10 cm³ of the water in a syringe and transfers this water to a Petri dish. She counts the water fleas in the dish. Further up the stream she sees many dead fish. How should she change her approach? Explain your reasoning.

Links

Learn about chance and probability ▶▶ **S29**

Primary data (or **primary evidence**) is data that you collect yourself by doing investigations. **Secondary data** (or **secondary evidence**) is data collected by other people.

Type of data	Advantages
Primary	You control the quality of the data
	You control what data is collected
	Up to date
	Relevant to your needs
Secondary	Quicker to obtain
	Easier to obtain
	Can be cheaper than setting up and running an experiment

Secondary data is usually found, together with a conclusion that someone has drawn from that data. You need to be careful because the data may have been manipulated to allow a certain conclusion to be drawn.

QUESTIONS

Level Booster

★★★ explain how data can be manipulated

★★ describe the link between some data and the conclusions drawn from it

★ identify different conclusions from a set of data

1 a ★ What is the difference between primary data and secondary data?

b ★ State two advantages of primary data.

2 Some factory workers collected this data about accidents in their factory. The data was then used in reports written by the factory owners and by the factory workers.

a ★ Did the workers or the factory owners use secondary data? Explain your answer.

b ★ One conclusion is that the factory is getting safer. Which set of data was used?

c ★ Another conclusion is that it is getting more dangerous. Which set of data was used?

d ★★ Suggest which conclusion the factory owners drew and why.

e ★★★ How would you manipulate the data to conclude that the number of accidents hasn't changed during the year?

Accidents...	Jan	Feb	Mar	Apr	May	Jun	Jul	Aug	Sep	Oct	Nov	Dec
...per month	20	20	15	15	20	21	14	20	23	12	20	26
...in 1st month of quarter	20			15			14			12		
...per quarter	55			56			57			58		

Links

Learn about evaluating data ▶▶ **S42**

A *symbol* is a way of representing something with a shape. A *convention* is a certain way of doing things. Scientists use conventions and symbols because they can:

* make it quicker to write things down
* make things look clearer
* be understood all over the world no matter what language is spoken.

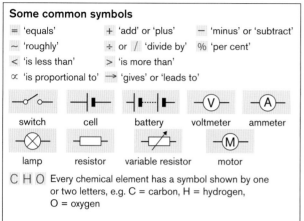

Some common symbols

$=$ 'equals'　　$+$ 'add' or 'plus'　　$-$ 'minus' or 'subtract'

$\sim$ 'roughly'　　$\div$ or $/$ 'divide by'　　$\%$ 'per cent'

$<$ 'is less than'　　$>$ 'is more than'

$\propto$ 'is proportional to'　　$\rightarrow$ 'gives' or 'leads to'

switch　　cell　　battery　　voltmeter　　ammeter

lamp　　resistor　　variable resistor　　motor

C H O　Every chemical element has a symbol shown by one or two letters, e.g. C = carbon, H = hydrogen, O = oxygen

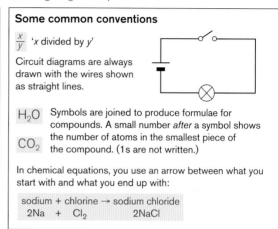

Some common conventions

$\frac{x}{y}$ '*x* divided by *y*'

Circuit diagrams are always drawn with the wires shown as straight lines.

H_2O　Symbols are joined to produce formulae for compounds. A small number *after* a symbol shows the number of atoms in the smallest piece of the compound. (1s are not written.)

CO_2

In chemical equations, you use an arrow between what you start with and what you end up with:

sodium + chlorine $\rightarrow$ sodium chloride
　2Na　 + 　Cl_2　　　　2NaCl

Figure A: Some common symbols and conventions used in science. There are more in the periodic table on page 100.

QUESTIONS

Level Booster

★★★ use a wide range of scientific symbols and conventions

★★ explain the importance of using symbols and conventions

★ use simple scientific symbols

1 ★ Write out these sentences using symbols:
 a five is greater than four
 b two plus two is equal to four
 c magnesium (Mg) and sulfur (S) react to make magnesium sulfide (MgS).

2 ★ Draw a circuit diagram to show two bulbs, an ammeter and a motor, all one after the other in the same circuit. The circuit is operated by a switch and contains a battery.

3 ★ Use the periodic table on page 100 to look up the names of the elements that have these symbols:
 a N; **b** Zn; **c** Rn; **d** W; **e** Au.

4 ★★ Write out question **1a** in words and its answer in symbols. Use the question and answer to help to explain the benefits of using symbols and conventions.

5 ★★ Look at the periodic table on page 100. Some elements, e.g. 118, do not have names yet and have three-letter codes instead. Suggest why it takes time for a new element to be given an official name.

6 ★★★ A chemical equation is 'balanced' if it has the same number of atoms of each element on either side of the arrow. Write out the chemical symbol equations for the following reactions.
 a hydrogen (H_2) and oxygen (O_2) react to make water
 b methane (CH_4) and oxygen react to make carbon dioxide and water
 c carbon dioxide and water react to make glucose ($C_6H_{12}O_6$) and oxygen
 d tin oxide (SnO_2) and hydrogen react to make tin and water

Links

Learn about the symbols for SI units ▶▶ **S6, S9**
Learn about mathematic symbols and conventions ▶▶ **S7, S8, S9, S10**
Learn about hazard symbols ▶▶ **S24**

Fractions

A **fraction** tells you how much of something you have. The 'thing' is divided into equal parts

One pizza …

… can be divided into any number of equal parts, but usually it's divided into 6.

$\overline{6}$

Two slices are eaten. There are now 4 parts out of a possible 6.

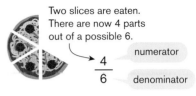

numerator

$\dfrac{4}{6}$

denominator

Figure A: Fractions

and the *total number* of equal parts goes on the bottom – this is the **denominator**. The *actual number* of parts that you have is put on the top – this is the **numerator**.

To simplify a fraction, you work out the largest number that divides exactly into *both* the numerator and the denominator – this is the highest common factor. You then divide the numerator and the denominator by this.

In science, we use scientific calculators to add, subtract, multiply or divide fractions. Make sure you have a calculator that can do this and that you know how to use it.

$\dfrac{4}{8}$
(four eighths)

The largest number that can exactly go into four and eight is four.

$\dfrac{1}{2}$
(one half)

÷4

$\dfrac{4}{8}$ → $\dfrac{1}{2}$

÷4

Figure B: Simplifying fractions.

Percentages

A **percentage** (%) is a fraction in which the denominator is 100. So 15% means '15 parts out of 100'. To show a fraction as a percentage, multiply it by 100. You should know by heart the relationships between some percentages and fractions, such as 50% = $\frac{1}{2}$, 25% = $\frac{1}{4}$ and 75% = $\frac{3}{4}$.

To calculate a percentage of a number, you multiply the number by the percentage (as a fraction or a decimal). For example, to calculate 9% of 2000, multiply 2000 by either $\frac{9}{100}$ or 0.09.

$\dfrac{5}{8} \times 100 = 0.625 \times 100 = 62.5\%$

To do this on a calculator:

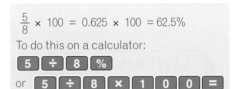

Figure C: Converting fractions to percentages.

To compare the size of one number with another, you divide one number by the other and multiply by 100. For example, if you want to know what percentage 6 is of 12, you write '6 of 12' as '$\frac{6}{12}$'.

Then, $\frac{6}{12} = \frac{1}{2}$ or 0.5. As a percentage 0.5 × 100 = 50%, so 6 is 50% of 12.

In science, you often need to find the percentage increase or percentage decrease of something.

A crucible and lid and a strip of magnesium had a mass of 15.40g. When heated, the magnesium reacted to leave a white powder in the crucible. The mass had increased to 15.45g. What was the percentage increase in mass?

Change in mass
= 15.45 − 15.40
= 0.05

change

Percentage change
= ($\dfrac{0.05}{15.4}$) × 100

starting value

= 0.3% increase

Some wood, with a mass of 2500g was burnt. The ash left at the end had a mass of 50g. What was the percentage decrease in mass?

Change in mass
= 2500 − 50
= 2450

change

Percentage change
= ($\dfrac{2450}{2500}$) × 100

starting value

= 98% decrease

Figure D: Calculating percentage increase and decrease.

To do this, you find the amount that something has changed by and then divide this by the starting value. You then multiply by 100. See figure D.

Ratios

A **ratio** compares two quantities. If Team A has 20 points and Team B has 30 points there is a '20 to 30 ratio', which is written as 20:30. You can simplify ratios in the same way that you simplify fractions – so, dividing both sides by 10, you get 2:3.

You can convert ratios into fractions to show how the first item compares with the second. In the example above the fraction is $\frac{2}{3}$, which means that Team A has two-thirds of the points of Team B. You can also use a fraction to compare how one item compares with the total. In this example, there are 50 points and Team A has $\frac{20}{30}$ or $\frac{2}{5}$ of the total number of points.

Decimals

A number that is not a **whole number** (**integer**) can be either a decimal or a fraction. A **decimal** is a line of digits. If there are no digits after the decimal point it's a whole number.

- To convert a fraction to a decimal, divide the numerator by the denominator.

$$\frac{3}{4} = 3 \div 4 = 0.75$$

- To convert a decimal to a fraction find out how many tenths, hundredths etc. there are after the decimal point and show these as a fraction.

$$2.4 \text{ is } 2 \text{ and } 4 \text{ tenths} = 2\frac{4}{10} = 2\frac{2}{5}$$

$$8.35 \text{ is } 8 \text{ and } 35 \text{ hundredths}$$
$$= 8\frac{35}{100} = 8\frac{7}{20}$$

Figure E: Converting decimals and fractions.

QUESTIONS

Level Booster

★★★ calculate percentage changes and compare ratios

★★ convert fractions to decimals, calculate percentages and simplify ratios

★ use fractions to explain what a percentage is, use ratios and use decimals

1 ★ Simplify these fractions:
 a $\frac{3}{12}$; b $\frac{36}{72}$; c $\frac{12}{54}$; d $\frac{9}{30}$.

2 ★ If 34% is written out as a fraction, what is the value of the denominator?

3 ★ The mass of an aluminium block is 14% of the mass of a gold block. Explain what this means without using the word 'percentage'.

4 ★ The ratio of hydrogen to oxygen atoms in water is 2:1. What does this mean?

5 ★ A carbon dioxide molecule contains 1 carbon atom and 2 oxygen atoms. What is the ratio of carbon atoms to oxygen atoms?

6 ★★ Convert these into decimals:
 a $\frac{1}{2}$; b $\frac{3}{4}$; c $\frac{34}{50}$; d $\frac{24}{60}$.

7 ★★ Convert the fractions in question **6** into percentages.

8 ★★ In a molecule of hydrogen peroxide there are two hydrogen atoms and two oxygen atoms. Write a simplified ratio to show how the numbers of these atoms compare.

9 ★★★ A piece of potato with mass 5.06 g was left in pure water for 12 hours. After this, its mass was 5.99 g. What was the percentage increase?

10 ★★★ Which of these ratios are equivalent? 3:2, 2:3, 4:5, 3:6, 32:64

Links

Learn about probability ▶▶ **S29**

An **average** is a single item used to represent all the other items in a set of data. There are three different types of average that you need to know about.

* The **mode** is the most common item in a set of data. It is the only average that can be used with items that are not numbers. See Figure A.

* The **median** is the middle value of a set of values, written in order. If there are two values in the middle then you add them together and divide by two. See Figure B.

* A **mean** is an average that takes all the values in a set of data into account. You add up all the values and divide by the number of values.

Means are affected by **outliers** (values far away from all the other values) but medians are not affected. See Figure C.

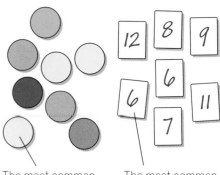

The most common colour is yellow. The mode is yellow.

The most common value is 6. The mode is 6.

Figure A: Finding a mode.

1 Put your values in order.

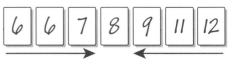

2 Count in from either end, one value at a time, until you are left with one or two values in the middle. In this case it is 8. The median is 8.

Figure B: Finding a median.

The sum of the values...

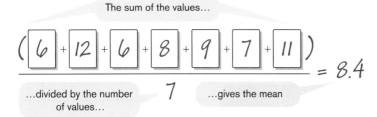

$$\frac{(6 + 12 + 6 + 8 + 9 + 7 + 11)}{7} = 8.4$$

...divided by the number of values...

...gives the mean

Figure C: Finding a mean.

QUESTIONS

Level Booster

★★★ select the best average to use in a particular situation

★★ calculate the mean of a set of data

★ find the mode and median of a set of data

1 Mrs Jones was sorting out lengths of tubing for a class practical. In the stock room she found the following lengths: 3 cm, 8 cm, 5 cm, 11 cm, 3 cm.
   a ★ What is the mode?
   b ★ What is the median?
   c ★★ Calculate the mean.

2 Graham measured the masses of some plant seedlings:
   16.0 g, 16.5 g, 18.5 g, 16.5 g, 17.8 g, 16.9 g, 16.8 g.

   a ★ What is the mode?
   b ★ What is the median?
   c ★★ Calculate the mean.

3 ★★★ Which average would you use for each of the following situations? Explain your reasoning in each case.
   a Identifying how many points a hotel must score to be called 'average' in a review of hotels.
   b Identifying the average height for a Year 9 boy.
   c Identifying the average popularity of singers among students at your school.

Links
Learn about percentages ▶▶ **S27**

There are six sides on a die, with a different number on each side. So, there are six possible numbers that can be thrown – each possibility is equally likely.

Throwing a die is a **random** process – you cannot predict which number will be thrown. So, we talk about the chance or **probability** of a certain number being thrown. The probability of throwing a four is 1 in 6. A probability can be written as a fraction, a decimal or a percentage.

We usually write probabilities as decimals on a scale of 0–1 (where 1 means it's certain that something will happen). The probabilities of all the possible outcomes always add up to 1. So, it follows that if there is a 0.17 chance of throwing a certain number on a die, there is a $1 - 0.17 = 0.83$ chance of *not* throwing that number.

There is a 1 in 6 chance of throwing a five. This can be written as a probability, which may be shown as a fraction, percentage or decimal with value 1 or less, in this case $\frac{1}{6}$ or 0.17 or 17%.

Figure A: Ways of writing probabilities.

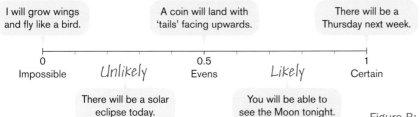

Figure B: The probability of scale.

QUESTIONS

Level Booster

★★★ use given probabilities to calculate other probabilities for the same outcome

★★ calculate the probability of an outcome not occurring

★ calculate and justify probabilities and use the probability scale

1 ★ There is an equally likely chance that a baby will be a boy or a girl. What is the probability of a couple having a boy? Give your answer in three different ways.

2 Jack plants one tulip bulb in a flowerpot. It is from a mixture in a bag that contains equal numbers of red, yellow, blue and purple tulips.
  a ★ Using the probability scale, what is the probability of planting a yellow tulip?
  b ★★ What is the probability of not planting a blue tulip?

3 Gina is doing a survey of a field. She has drawn a plan of the field and drawn a grid to divide it into 25 equal sized squares. She has lettered the squares from A to Y and written the letters on pieces of paper, which she has put in a box.
  a ★ What is the probability that she draws out the letter 'X' first?
  b ★★ What is the probability that she does not draw out the letter 'T' first?
  c ★★★ What is the probability that she draws out a letter from A–E first?
  d ★★★ What is the probability that she draws out 25 pieces of paper in 25 turns?

Links

Learn about fractions, decimals and percentages
▶▶ **S27**

Tables are used to record data. When this data records the numbers of times results happen, it is a **frequency table** or **frequency diagram**.

You should always design a table when planning an investigation because it helps you to think about:
* what variables to choose
* the range of measurements to use
* the intervals to have between measurements
* how to make your measurements.

Tables are used to present small sets of data because they let you sort the data into different orders (e.g. increasing number, alphabetically). This helps you to spot patterns.

There is a standard way of setting out a table.

the variable you select values for (the **independent variable)**

the variable you measure (the **dependent variable)**

Time (mins)	Temperature of water (°C)
0	24.0
1	31.1
2	38.7
3	46.3
4	54.2
5	62.1

interval

range

Figure B: Temperature of 300 cm³ of water heated for different lengths of time.

discrete variable   frequency

Flavour of crisps	Students in 11 F with that favourite	Students in 11 B with that favourite
cheese & onion	6	9
other	1	3
prawn cocktail	2	2
ready salted	7	3
salt & vinegar	11	8
smoky bacon	3	2

Continuous data is often put into groups. You need to make sure that your groups:
* are all the same size (so you can make comparisons)
* do not overlap (otherwise you have more than one choice of group to put a reading into).

Height groups (cm)	4 year olds with that height
90.0 – 94.9	1
95.0 – 99.9	3
100.0 – 104.9	7
105.0 – 109.9	8
110.0 – 114.9	1

Figure A: Frequency tables.

QUESTIONS

Level Booster

★★★ draw tables to help plan investigations

★★ draw tables for continuous data and group continuous data where necessary

★ draw frequency tables for discrete data

1 ★ Look at the crisp-flavour frequency data for class 11F, in Figure A. Draw a frequency table for this data, but order the data by the popularity of the flavours.

2 A survey of rabbits on a hill and their heights above sea level produced this data:
Rabbit A (499 m), B (300 m), C (246 m), D (434 m), E (302 m), F (458 m), G (255 m), H (365 m), I (299 m), J (249 m), K (355 m), L (258 m).
a ★★ Is there is a range of heights in which more rabbits are found? Draw a suitable table to find out.
b ★★★ How does drawing a table make it easier to spot patterns, compared to having a list?

3 Look at Figure B.
a ★ State the choices of range, interval and variables used in the experiment.
b ★★★ What trend can you see?

Links
Learn about variables ▶▶ **S13**
Learn about other ways of presenting data ▶▶ **S38**

Bar charts are used to present data.

✖ The **independent variable** is **qualitative** or **quantitative** *and* **discrete.**
✖ The **dependent variable** is **quantitative**.

Always give your charts a title.

The variable that you measure (dependent variable) goes on the vertical axis. Give the name and units.

Choose a scale so that the bars fill as much of the graph paper as possible. Number the scale and remember that the intervals must be equal.

The variable that you change (independent variable) goes on the horizontal axis. Write in its name.

Temperature increase of 300 cm³ of water heated for 2 minutes by burning 30 cm³ of different types of wood.

Gaps are left between the bars to make it easier to read.

Bars are drawn:
• with a ruler
• from each category up to the correct level
• with equal widths
This bar tells you that pine raised the temperature of the water by 30 °C.

Figure A: A bar chart.

Generally the independent variable is plotted on the horizontal axis (*x*-axis). The dependent variable is plotted on the vertical axis (*y*-axis). It can be done the other way around but the bars always 'come out of' which ever axis the independent variable is plotted on.

To show how several of the same things change in different groups, you group the bars.

Make the bars for the different things different colours or patterns.

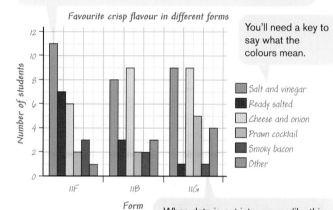

You'll need a key to say what the colours mean.

- Salt and vinegar
- Ready salted
- Cheese and onion
- Prawn cocktail
- Smoky bacon
- Other

Figure B: A bar chart with bars in groups.

When data is put into groups like this, we don't leave gaps between the bars.

QUESTIONS

Level Booster

★★★ explain how using bar charts allows better spotting of patterns

★★ draw a bar chart

★ read from a bar chart and spot patterns in bar charts

1 Look at Figure A. To the nearest degree, by how much did the following woods raise the temperature of the water:
a ★ pine
b ★ cedar?

2 ★★ An experiment was done in which the amount of vitamin C in 100 g of different fruits was measured: mango (37 mg), kiwi fruit (59 mg), apple (6 mg), grapefruit (31 mg), banana (11 mg), grape (11 mg), blackberry (6 mg), orange (54 mg). Plot this data on a bar chart.

3 Look at Figure B.
a ★ What is the independent variable in this survey?
b ★★★ What are the two most popular flavours of crisps?
c ★★★ Explain why it is easier to spot these using the bar chart rather than the table in Figure A on page 36 in S30.

Links

Learn about types of data ▶▶ **S5**
Learn about variables ▶▶ **S13**
Learn about other ways of presenting data ▶▶ **S38**

A **frequency diagram** is a table, chart or graph that shows the numbers of things (their **frequency**). They may look like bar charts or line graphs.

A **histogram** is a type of frequency diagram that is drawn when the independent variable has **continuous data** that has been grouped together.

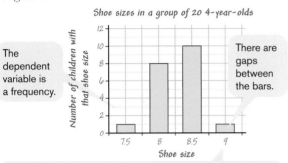

The dependent variable is a frequency.

There are gaps between the bars.

The groups are of discrete data (shoes only come in certain sizes).

Figure A: A frequency diagram (in the form of a bar chart).

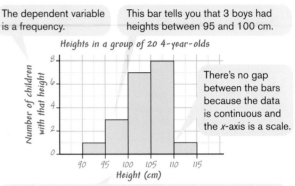

The dependent variable is a frequency.

This bar tells you that 3 boys had heights between 95 and 100 cm.

There's no gap between the bars because the data is continuous and the x-axis is a scale.

This independent variable is continuous data. To draw a histogram we need to group it. The scale shows that the boundaries between the groups are 95, 100, 105 and 110. If you are drawing a histogram you must decide which group should include the boundary value.

Figure B: A histogram.

QUESTIONS

Level Booster

★★★ decide to draw a histogram when appropriate

★★ draw a histogram

★ draw a bar chart frequency diagram and read from a histogram

1 a ★ Convert the data in the frequency diagram and histogram above into the tables.
   b What does the dependent variable measure in a histogram?

2 ★ Old Faithful is a geyser in Yellowstone National Park in America. At regular intervals it shoots hot water and steam out of the ground. What does the histogram in Figure C tell you about the geyser?

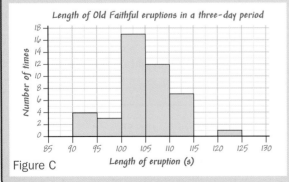

Figure C

3 ★ The numbers of passengers on the number 391 bus were counted at a certain bus stop during one afternoon. It contained 1–5 people 2 times, 6–10 people 12 times, 11–15 people 13 times and 16–20 people 4 times. Plot this data on a frequency diagram.

4 ★★ A council must reduce the height of any trees that are over 20 m tall along Plane Road. It wants to know how many trees will need cutting this year and how many will need cutting in 5 years' time (trees that are currently 18–20 m tall). The heights (in metres) of the trees are: 15.0, 16.2, 21.2, 20.2, 15.4, 22.1, 19.5, 21.0, 18.9, 19.2, 20.1, 17.3, 19.2, 17.5, 18.1, 15.3. Present the data in a form that make it easy for the council to see how many trees to cut.

5 ★★★ The boss of a company wants to know the number of people doing each different job in her company. She also wants to know how many people are earning certain amounts of money in the company (in all jobs). What chart or graph would you use to present each of these sets of data? Explain your choice(s).

Links

Learn about continuous and discrete data ▶▶ **S5**
Learn about variables ▶▶ **S13**
Learn about other ways of presenting data ▶▶ **S38**

Line graphs are used to present data when both the **independent variable** and the **dependent variable** are in the form of **quantitative data**. They are used to show how one variable changes with another. The independent variable is often time.

The independent variable is plotted on the horizontal axis (*x*-axis). The dependent variable is plotted on the vertical axis (*y*-axis).

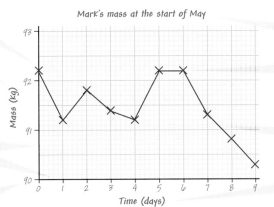

Graphs don't have to start at 0.

Dependent variable Write in its name and units.

Choose scales for your axes so that the points fill as much of the graph paper as possible. Number the scales and remember that the intervals must be equal.

The axes don't need to start at 0.

Always give your graphs a title.

Plot each point, in pencil, with a neat ×. Then connect the points with straight lines, using a ruler.

Line graphs can be used to **estimate** new values. We estimate that after 6.5 days Mark had a mass of 91.75 kg.

Independent variable Write in its name and units.

Figure A: A line graph.

QUESTIONS

Level Booster

★★★ decide to draw a line graph instead of a bar chart or histogram

★★ draw a line graph

★ read from a line graph

1 Look at the line graph in Figure B.

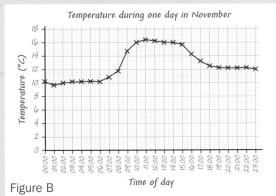

Figure B

a ★ What is the independent variable and what is the dependent variable on this graph?

b ★ What intervals is the *y*-axis scale marked up in?

c ★ How many °C does each of the little squares represent on the *y*-axis?

d ★ What is the maximum temperature shown?

e ★ What is the minimum temperature shown?

f ★★ Estimate the temperature at 08:30.

2 a ★★ The pressure in blood vessels just after the heart has pumped blood into them is called the systolic blood pressure. It is often measured in 'millimetres of mercury' (mmHg). An experiment was done on some female marathon runners to see how their systolic blood pressure changed after 30 minutes on a treadmill. Readings were taken at intervals and means were calculated: after 0 mins (178 mmHg), after 3 mins (136), 5 mins (119), 10 mins (108), 20 mins (105), 30 mins (104). Plot this data on a line graph.

b ★★★ Explain why this data is best displayed as a line graph and not a bar chart or histogram.

Links

Learn about continuous and discrete data ▶▶ **S5**
Learn about estimating ▶▶ **S11**
Learn about variables ▶▶ **S13**
Learn about other ways of presenting data ▶▶ **S38**

Scatter graphs are used when you want to find a **correlation** (a link) between two numerical variables.

You use a line graph to see how a variable changes, usually with time. You use a scatter graph to try to find evidence that one variable is having an effect on the other.

A **line of best fit** is often drawn through the points on a scatter graph. The line goes through the middle of the points, so that about half the points are on either side of it. You ignore any **anomalous data (outliers)** when drawing a line of best fit.

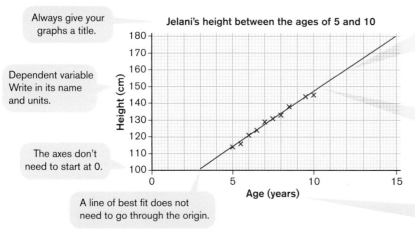

Always give your graphs a title.

Dependent variable Write in its name and units.

The axes don't need to start at 0.

A line of best fit does not need to go through the origin.

Extending the line of best fit allows us to estimate other values outside our data.

line of best fit – drawn with a ruler!

Independent variable Write in its name and units.

Jelani's height between the ages of 5 and 10

Figure A: This line of best fit shows a correlation between Jelani's height and his age.

QUESTIONS

Level Booster

★★★ decide to draw a scatter graph instead of a line graph and draw a line of best fit

★★ draw a scatter graph

★ read from a scatter graph and identify trends in a scatter graph

1 Look at the scatter graph in Figure A.
  a ★What are the independent and dependent variables on this graph?
  b ★What intervals is the *y*-axis scale marked up in?
  c ★What is the correlation (link) between Jelani's age and his height?
  d ★★Estimate Jelani's height at age 12.

2 The table shows the distances of the four inner planets from the Sun, and how long it takes each one to orbit (go around) the Sun.

Planet	Distance from Sun (million km)	Time for one orbit of the Sun (Earth days)
Mercury	58	88
Venus	108	225
Earth	150	365
Mars	228	687

  a ★★Plot this data on a scatter graph.
  b ★★What correlation (link) can you see?
  c ★★★ Draw a line of best fit through the points on your scatter graph.

3 ★★★ Explain why you would use a scatter graph for the data in question **2**, instead of a line graph.

Links

Learn about correlations ▶▶ **S15**
Learn about gradients ▶▶ **S35**
Learn about other ways of presenting data ▶▶ **S38**

Lines on graphs can be used to:
- ✳ estimate other values within your data
- ✳ estimate other values outside your data
- ✳ calculate the **gradient** of a line – the resulting units will be the vertical axis units divided by the horizontal axis units
- ✳ see if two variables are directly proportional.

Straight lines that go through the origin show variables that are **directly proportional**. This means that when one variable changes, the other changes in the same way by the same percentage. For example, in Figure A when the distance doubles, the time also doubles.

EXTENSION The equation of a graph showing direct proportion is $y = mx$, where 'm' is the gradient. If the line does not go through the origin, the variables are not directly proportional and the equation is $y = mx + c$, where 'c' is the value at which the line crosses the y-axis.

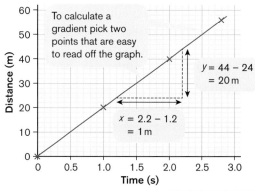

Distance covered by a hovercar just after taking off

To calculate a gradient pick two points that are easy to read off the graph.

$y = 44 - 24$
$= 20\,m$

$x = 2.2 - 1.2$
$= 1\,m$

gradient = y/x
$= 20/1$
$= 20\,m/s$
So, in this case the gradient is the speed

Figure A: The gradient of a line contains valuable information.

QUESTIONS

Level Booster

★★★ work out the gradient of a line and build equations for lines on graphs

★★ identify variables that are directly proportional

★ recognise that straight-line graphs can be expressed in equations

1 Look Figure A on page 40 in S34.
  a ★Estimate Jelani's height at 9 years old and at 12 years old.
  b ★★Calculate the gradient of the line.
  c ★★What are the units for this gradient?
  d ★★ Is age directly proportional to height? Explain your reasoning.

2 Look Figure A on this page.
  a ★★ Are the two variables directly proportional? Explain your reasoning.
  b ★★★ State the equation for this line, in terms of x and y.

3 Figure B shows the relationship between the Celsius temperature scale and the older Fahrenheit scale.

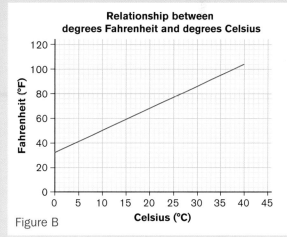

Figure B

  a ★★ Are the two variables directly proportional? Explain your reasoning.
  b ★★★ State the equation for this line.

Links
Learn about scatter graphs ▶▶ **S34**

Pie charts are used to compare the contributions made to something by different categories. A pie chart is a circle and the angle at the centre is 360°. These 360° are divided up in the same proportions as the different categories.

It is often difficult to compare one pie chart with another, and a grouped bar chart is better to use when you want make comparisons.

Figure A: Constructing a pie chart.

Favourite flavour of crisps	Number of students in class 11F
cheese & onion	6
other	1
prawn cocktail	2
ready salted	7
salt & vinegar	11
smoky bacon	3

Step 1: Find the total number.
total is 30

Step 2: Divide 360° by the total number.
360/30 = 12 (so each student is represented by 12° of the circle)

Step 3: Multiply the number in each category by your answer to step 2.
e.g. 6 × 12° = 72°

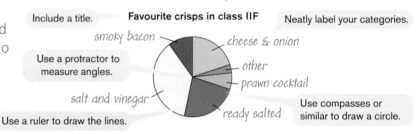

Include a title.
Neatly label your categories.
Use a protractor to measure angles.
Use a ruler to draw the lines.
Use compasses or similar to draw a circle.

Favourite crisps in class 11F

QUESTIONS

Level Booster

★★★ decide to construct a pie chart rather than a bar chart for categorical data

★★ calculate the angles needed to construct pie charts

★ interpret and construct pie charts when given the angles

1 ★ Look at the pie chart in Figure A. How can you tell that salt & vinegar was the most popular flavour of crisps?

2 ★ The table shows the uses of electricity in an average house in the UK. Display the data as a pie chart.

Use	Computers & appliances	Lighting	Fridge & freezer	Cooking	TV, video & audio	Washing, drying
Percentage	12%	20%	17%	16%	20%	15%
Angle on pie chart	43°	72°	61°	58°	72°	54°

3 ★★ Air contains 78.1% nitrogen, 21.0% oxygen and the rest is other gases. Display this data on a pie chart.

4 ★★ A survey of 90 adults was done to find out how much time they spent on the internet each day: 3 of them spent over 7 hours a day online, 17 were online for between 3 and 7 hours, 33 used the internet for 1–3 hours and 37 used it for less than an hour. Display this data as a pie chart.

5 ★★★ The pie charts in Figure B have been drawn to show how energy use in Scotland has changed. Why would it be better to show this data as a grouped bar chart?

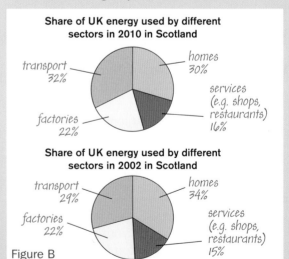

Share of UK energy used by different sectors in 2010 in Scotland

transport 32%
homes 30%
services (e.g. shops, restaurants) 16%
factories 22%

Share of UK energy used by different sectors in 2002 in Scotland

transport 29%
homes 34%
services (e.g. shops, restaurants) 15%
factories 22%

Figure B

Links

Learn about other ways of presenting data ▶▶ **S38**

Venn diagrams are used to show associations between different sets of things. Each set is shown as a loop, such as a circle or an oval.

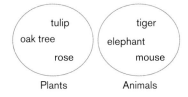

Plants   Animals

Figure A: No members of one set belong to the other.

Words meaning 'hello'   Words meaning 'goodbye'

Figure B: If two groups share items then the ovals overlap. These two sets share some items.

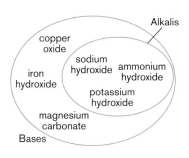

Figure C: If one set of things is found entirely inside a bigger set, you show one oval inside another. One group is a subset of another.

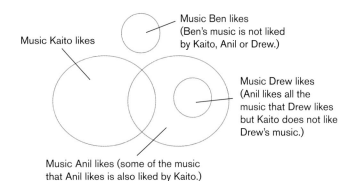

Music Kaito likes

Music Ben likes (Ben's music is not liked by Kaito, Anil or Drew.)

Music Drew likes (Anil likes all the music that Drew likes but Kaito does not like Drew's music.)

Music Anil likes (some of the music that Anil likes is also liked by Kaito.)

Figure D: You can use different Venn diagrams together. This Venn diagram showing the associations between the music liked by four boys.

QUESTIONS

Level Booster

★★★ construct Venn diagrams using a combination of overlaps and subsets

★★ construct Venn diagrams using overlaps or subsets

★ interpret Venn diagrams

1 ★ Describe in words what the Venn diagrams in Figures A, B and C tell you.

2 ★ Look at Figure D. What does the Venn diagram tell you about the music Kaito likes and the music Drew likes?

3 ★★ A daffodil grows from a bulb and has a stem, leaves and roots. A cactus has a stem, roots and spikes. Draw a Venn diagram to compare the two plants.

4 a ★★ Outline a Venn diagram to show that all mammals are animals.
   b ★★ Add birds to your diagram.

5 ★★★ Divide the liquids in the list below into sets 'thick liquids', 'liquids people consume', 'liquids that contain alcohol': beer, engine oil, gloss paint, honey, ketchup, orange juice, red wine, water. Then draw a Venn diagram to show these sets.

6 ★★★ The British Isles consists of various islands including the Isle of Man, Ireland and Great Britain (the island that contains England, Scotland and Wales).
The island of Ireland contains the Republic of Ireland and Northern Ireland. Northern Ireland is a part of the United Kingdom along with Great Britain. Show this information on a Venn diagram.

Links

Learn about other ways of presenting data ▶▶ **S38**

The table shows when you need to use the different charts, graphs and diagrams.

Presentation type	Independent variable	Dependent variable	Used ...	Skill
Table	qualitative or quantitative	qualitative or quantitative	to record data and put it in order	S30
Bar chart	qualitative or quantitative, discrete	quantitative	to compare differences	S31
Frequency diagram	qualitative or quantitative	quantitative (frequency)	to show the number of times something occurs	S32
Histogram	quantitative, continuous (grouped)	quantitative (frequency)	to show the number of times something occurs	S32
Line graph	quantitative, continuous (usually time)	quantitative	normally to show how something changes with time	S33
Scatter graph	quantitative	quantitative	to find relationships between variables	S34
Pie chart	to compare the contributions of things to a whole			S36
Venn diagram	to show associations between different groups			S37
Flow chart	to show how one part of a process follows another			S1

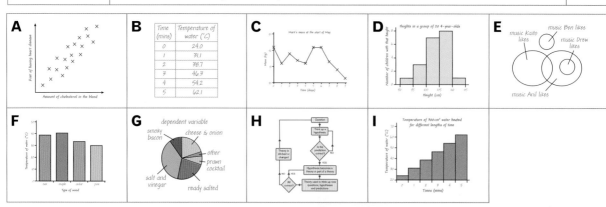

QUESTIONS

Level Booster

- ★★★ justify the choice of how data is presented
- ★★ choose the most appropriate diagram, chart or graph
- ★ recognise the different sorts of diagrams, charts and graphs

1 ★ Refer to the table above. Identify the type of diagram, chart or graph shown below it.

2 ★★ Present the data in question **2** on page 36 in S30 in an appropriate way.

3 a ★★★ Look at the table for crisp flavours in Figure A on page 38 in S30. Suggest three ways of presenting this data and explain which would be best for seeing the favourite flavours.

b ★★★ Look at the other two tables in Figures A and B on page 38 in S30. How would you present each set of data? Justify your choices.

S39 DRAWING CONCLUSIONS

A **conclusion** is a decision made after looking at evidence – such as the results of an investigation.

QWC A conclusion section in an investigation report must be organised to make it easy to follow. You could use the writing frame below.

✱ State what you have found out.

✱ State why you think this happens – your **hypothesis**.

✱ Explain how your results support your findings.

✱ Say whether your findings agree with your **prediction** or describe how they differ.

I have found out that...

My idea is that... depends on...

My results show that...

My findings agree/disagree with my prediction.

Your conclusion must:

✱ Be **valid** – which means that it must be drawn from the results.
✱ Not say things that cannot be worked out from the results.
✱ Use scientific words.

QWC Use connectives to join your phrases together – such as 'because', 'so', 'this causes', 'therefore', 'while', 'after that', 'next'.

QUESTIONS

Level Booster

★★★ suggest how evidence can be explained using different hypotheses

★★ explain how evidence supports or does not support a conclusion

★ compare a prediction with the results in an investigation

1 **QWC** ★ Kenny's conclusion states: 'My prediction was that if the car is on a smoother slope then it will go faster. The wood was the smoothest surface. The car went 2 m/s on the wooden surface, which is faster than on the other surfaces. This was because there is less friction on smoother surfaces. My prediction was right. The car goes fastest on the smoothest surface.' Rearrange the sentences to improve this conclusion.

2 Mia burnt different types of wood and measured the temperature increase of some water. She predicted that if she burnt the same volume of each wood, the temperature rise would be the same. Her results are shown in Figure A on page 37 in S31.

 a ★ How does her prediction compare with her results?

 b ★★ Part of Mia's conclusion reads: 'So it's not volume that matters, but how heavy the wood is. The heavier the wood, the more it makes the water heat up.' Is this a good conclusion? Explain your reasoning.

3 ★★★ During the last year the number of reported crimes in Town X has risen. Suggest two different reasons why this might have happened.

4 ★★★ The numbers of a certain bird were recorded in some farmland each year. The numbers started to decrease each year after the farmer began putting poison down each spring. Suggest hypotheses to explain the decrease in bird numbers.

Links

Learn about hypotheses ▶▶ **S3**
Learn about validity ▶▶ **S21**
Learn about arguments ▶▶ **S41**

A **model** is anything that represents a thing or a process in a way that makes it easier to understand. Models are particularly useful when thinking about and explaining processes that you cannot see.

For example, DNA is a molecule found in cells. We cannot see it but physical models (that you can touch) help in understanding what it is made of and how it works.

Models can also be abstract (be a way of thinking). DNA contains the instructions for cells, so DNA is like an instruction manual – that's an abstract model.

Models simplify the real nature of something. We usually choose as simple a model as possible – one that is 'good enough' to use for a certain explanation.

We model particles in the kinetic theory (see S4) as being like tiny round balls. Particles are not quite like this but the model is good enough to use to explain what happens when materials change between solids, liquids and gases.

The model of DNA as an instruction manual is good enough to explain the function of DNA, but not good enough to explain how DNA actually works.

Investigations can be used to create new models and to test existing models. Models can also be used to think up **hypotheses** and to make **predictions**.

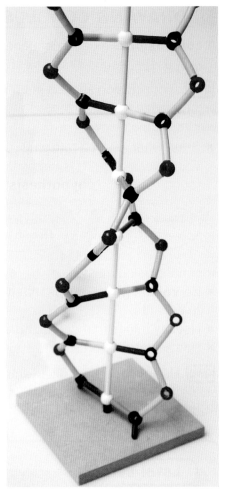

Figure A: A physical model of DNA.

A chemical equation has an arrow:

$$\text{hydrogen} + \text{oxygen} \rightarrow \text{water}$$

What you start with   the arrow means 'goes to give'   What you end up with

Figure B: Equations and formulae are abstract models.

A mathematical formula usually has an equals sign:

$$\text{speed} = \frac{\text{distance}}{\text{time}}$$

$$S = \frac{D}{T}$$

We can use letters instead of words to make things clearer.

$$S = \frac{30\,\text{m}}{10\,\text{s}}$$

If we know the distance (D) and the time taken to cover that distance (T), we can work out the speed (S).

$$S = 3\,\text{m/s}$$

S is the 'subject' of the formula but we can change this by rearranging. When you move something across the equals sign, it changes to its opposite. So moving 'divided by T' across the equals sign becomes 'multiplied by T'. If you move $+x$ it becomes $-x$.

$$S \times T = D$$

This is the same as $D = S \times T$ or $D = ST$. D is now the subject.

1 a ★ Light travels in a straight line. How could you use string as a model for this?

b ★ The planets go round the Sun. How could you use some balls to model this?

c ★ Particles in a gas are spread out. How could you use some balls to model this?

d ★★ Why do models like this help you to understand the nature of light, planets and particles?

2 ★ A car travels 21 m in 7 seconds. How fast is it going? Show your working.

3 a ★ When sodium reacts with chlorine, sodium chloride is formed. Write a word equation to model this reaction.

b ★★ Suggest something that this model is not good enough to do when we think about the reaction between sodium and chlorine.

4 ★★ The particles in a gas are moving. The model in question **1c** does not show this. Is that model good enough to explain why gases can be squashed? Explain your reasoning.

5 Figure C shows an electric circuit. Figures D and E show two different models used to think about how an electric circuit works.

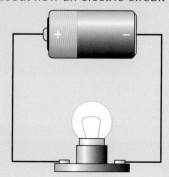

Figure C: An electric circuit.

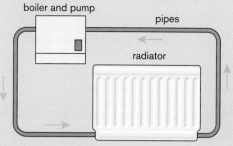

Figure D: A way of thinking about electric circuits – a central heating system.

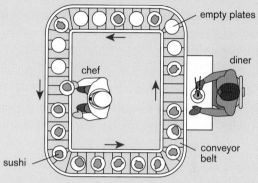

Figure E: A way of thinking about electric circuits – a food conveyer.

a ★★ Draw a table to compare how the models shown in Figures D and E represent the parts of the electric circuit shown in Figure C.

b ★★★ List the strengths and weaknesses of the two models.

6 ★★★ The angle at which light hits a flat surface equals the angle at which it leaves.

a Why is throwing table tennis balls at a flat surface a better model than using string?

b In what way is the table tennis model not so good?

7 ★★★ As your heart pumps, muscles in the top chambers relax to allow blood in. They then squeeze blood from the top chambers into the lower chambers and relax again. As they relax, muscles in the bottom chambers contract and squeeze blood out of the heart. What are the strengths and weaknesses of using a bicycle pump to model the heart?

8 ★★★ A train goes at a speed of 204 km/h for 15 minutes. What distance does it travel? Show your working.

Links

Learn about hypotheses and predictions ▶▶ **S3**

QWC An **argument** is a way of telling people what you think and why. Arguments may contain persuasive language – such as repeating evidence, exaggerating, using the pronoun 'we', asking the reader questions and using strong, descriptive words (emotive language).

QWC An argument must have evidence (reasons why you think the way you do). A good argument will also have a clear structure. Use this writing frame to help you:

✱ Make a statement of what you think (your **opinion**).

✱ Give your first reason for why you think this, with supporting evidence (you can use evidence selectively, choosing only parts that support your opinion.) You can introduce evidence using phrases such as 'Research has shown …', 'Scientists suggest …' and 'Studies have demonstrated …'.

✱ Give your other reasons (one paragraph per reason).

✱ Write a summary, in which you state your opinion again.

EXTENSION Better arguments include a **counterclaim** or **counterargument**. This is an explanation of why others may not agree with you and the evidence they have. You then write a response to the counterargument to explain why you are still right.

The Earth is round like a ball …

… because during a lunar eclipse you always see a circular shadow of the Earth on the Moon. The only shape that always makes a circular shadow, no matter what way round it is, is a sphere.

But that bloke Eusebios will say that the Earth is flat because you can't see beyond the horizon.

If the Earth were flat, ships would fall off the edge. But ships go over the horizon and come back. This is further evidence that the Earth is a sphere.

Figure A: An argument.

QUESTIONS

Level Booster

★★★ construct an argument including a counterargument

★★ construct an argument supported by evidence

★ select information to support a viewpoint

1 a **QWC** ★ Which of the following sentences would you use to support the use of animals in circus shows?
A In the wild a tiger has a home territory of about 20 km^2.
B The animals can get the right amount of healthy food.
C A vet gives the animals excellent medical care.
D Why not let children have a chance to appreciate beautiful animals up close?

E Animals perform degrading and unnatural tricks.

b **QWC** ★★ Why are the last two statements persuasive?

c **QWC** ★★ Write an argument in favour of or against the use of animals in circus shows.

2 **QWC** ★★★ The average cost of a Key Stage 3 boy's school uniform in the UK is £28. For girls it is £31.78. Write an argument in favour of school uniform. Include three key reasons, and remember that each reason needs its own paragraph with supporting evidence.

3 **QWC** ★★★ Look at the newspaper report in Figure A on page 58 in S48. Identify the counterargument and the response to this counterargument.

Links

Learn about conclusions ▶▶ **S39**

S42 EVALUATING

An **evaluation** is a summary of how well something does its job. Different parts of an investigation can be evaluated.

QWC When writing an evaluation you can use the bulleted lists below as writing frames.

Evaluate the results **QWC**

- Do the results let you answer the question? (Is the investigation **valid**?)
- Do they measure what they were supposed to? (Are the actual results valid?)
- Were there lots of **anomalous results**?
- How **repeatable** or **reproducible** are the results?
- Have the results been collected in an unbiased way? (Or is there **bias** in the method that shifts the results in a certain direction?)

Evaluate the conclusion **QWC**

- Were there enough results to draw a **conclusion** that you can be sure of?
- Has the conclusion been drawn from only the results? (Is it valid?)
- Is the conclusion unbiased? (Is it trying to persuade you that the results show something that they don't really show?)

You should try to **justify** your answers.

QUESTIONS

Level Booster

★★★ evaluate a conclusion, including making sure that there is no bias

★★ evaluate a set of results

★ describe how a certain conclusion has been based on evidence

1 Fouad wanted to know if there was a temperature increase when iron reacts with an acid. He put three rusty nails of the same type in different test tubes and added the same amount of acid to each. After 30 seconds, thermometers showed temperature increases of 0.2, 0.1 and 2 degrees Celsius.

He concluded that the reaction between iron and the acid causes a temperature increase.

a ★ Describe how Fouad has reached his conclusion.

b **QWC** ★★ Evaluate the results, suggesting any improvements to his method.

c **QWC** ★★★ Evaluate Fouad's conclusion.

Links

Learn about precision and accuracy ▶▶ **S16**
Learn about anomalous results ▶▶ **S19**
Learn about validity ▶▶ **S21**
Learn about repeatability and reliability ▶▶ **S22**
Learn about conclusions ▶▶ **S39**

QWC Scientists tell others about their ideas by giving talks at conferences and/or writing **papers**. A paper uses a similar writing frame to an investigation report:

* abstract – an overview of the hypothesis tested and the results
* introduction – discusses the existing evidence that supports the hypothesis
* methods – what was done and how it was done
* results – the data collected during the investigation
* conclusion – what the results show and whether or not they support the hypothesis
* references – the names of the papers, websites etc. used to write the paper.

A paper is sent to a **journal** (a magazine for scientific papers).

The editors of journals send papers that look interesting to experts in the subjects covered in the papers. These expert scientists **evaluate** the investigations. They check that the stated **conclusions** can be drawn from the results and that any opinions are supported by the evidence. They then say whether the paper should be published or if changes are needed. This is called **peer review**.

The expert scientists may not agree with the conclusions in a paper because different scientists often develop different ideas to explain the same data. Only further experiments can settle the matter but the paper can still be published.

A reviewing scientist checks that the results are not **biased** (shifted in a certain direction). Poor investigation design or poor measuring can cause bias. However, sometimes scientists use bias on purpose to:

* please people who employ them
* become famous
* make money.

A **theory** is not discarded until a new theory has been developed that fully explains all the observations. This involves many investigations and papers – not just one (which may be biased or contain **anomalous results**). Scientists tend not to believe evidence that is not **repeatable** or **reproducible**. However, evidence may be given more importance if it comes from a famous or well-respected scientist.

Figure A: The journal *Science* comes out every week.

scientist sends paper to journal

checked by editor and sent to other scientists for comments

based on feedback from the scientists, the editor decides whether to publish

Figure B: The peer review process.

Level Booster

★★★ describe the peer review process

★★ recognise that the views of different scientists hold different weights

★ organise information into an investigation report

1 **[QWC]** ★ The following are extracts from an investigation report, which had no abstract. In which section of the investigation report does each extract belong?

a 'Textbooks state that less current will flow through resistance wire than through normal copper wire of the same thickness and length.'

b 'The longer the wire, the smaller the current.'

c 'Collins New GCSE Science for AQA'

d 'Three lengths of resistance wire (10 cm, 30 cm, 50 cm)'

e

Wire length (cm)	Current (A)
10	0.38
30	0.20
50	0.12

2 ★ Suggest one reason why all scientific papers should be written using the same format.

3 ★★ Abstracts are freely available on the internet.

a Give one reason why an abstract is useful.

b **[QWC]** Write an abstract for the investigation in question **1**, using one sentence.

4 ★ How are the results and conclusion sections of an investigation report different?

5 Fossils of large, plant-eating *Tenontosaurus* dinosaurs are often found together with smaller, meat-eating *Velociraptor* fossils. One scientist says this is because *Velociraptors* were scavengers. They waited for a predator to kill a larger dinosaur before they fed on the meat left over. Another scientist says that *Velociraptors* hunted in packs and killed *Tenontosaurus* dinosaurs. And another scientist says that *Velociraptors* were afraid of *Tenontosaurus* dinosaurs.

a ★ How many different opinions are there?

b ★★ Which opinion(s) are not supported by evidence?

6 Chlorophyll from plants contains a lot of magnesium. According to TV nutritionist Gillian McKeith this means that: 'in the heart chlorophyll aids in the transmission of nerve impulses that control contraction … each contraction is increased in power.' The evidence for this statement comes from *Earthletter* magazine. Professor Christopher Fry wrote a paper for the *American Journal of Physiology* in which he says: 'An increase in magnesium concentration is also negatively inotropic.' Something that is negatively inotropic weakens the force of muscles.

a ★★ Which statement do you think holds more weight, and why?

b ★★ Gillian McKeith took a non-medical course that allowed her to put the title 'Doctor' in front of her name. After complaints she agreed to stop using 'doctor' in her adverts. Why do you think she wanted to use 'doctor'?

c ★★★ Describe the process that Professor Fry's results and conclusions have gone through before being published.

Links

Learn about conclusions ▶▶ **S39**

Learn about bias ▶▶ **S12, S16, S17**

Learn about repeatability and reliability ▶▶ **S22**

Learn about evaluating ▶▶ **S42**

S44 BENEFITS, DRAWBACKS AND IMPLICATIONS

New technologies have **benefits**, **drawbacks** and **implications**. A benefit is a good thing that comes from something. The opposite of a benefit is a drawback. An implication is a knock-on effect of doing something. It describes how doing one thing will then lead to other things happening.

Figure A: Some benefits, drawbacks and implications of installing a Wi-Fi network.

Benefits	you can use the internet without needing wires	you can use the internet wherever you like
Drawbacks	expense	other devices can interfere with its signal reducing the speed of the internet connection.
Implications	encourages more people to use the internet.	

If you are asked to evaluate (judge) the benefits, drawbacks and implications of something, it is good idea to think of some **criteria** to use. Examples of criteria include how many people are affected, how much it costs and how likely it is to happen.

Managers and doctors in a hospital need to decide how money is spent. They will use the techniques that are best suited to patients but they try to make sure that they do not spend more money on a patient than is necessary. It would not be sensible to give an expensive CT scan to someone with a suspected broken leg. Doctors would first use a cheaper way of investigating the leg, such as taking an X-ray photograph or using ultrasound. Only if the break was found to be very complicated would they then need to use a more expensive method to look at it. Figures B–D show some techniques that doctors can use to see inside patients.

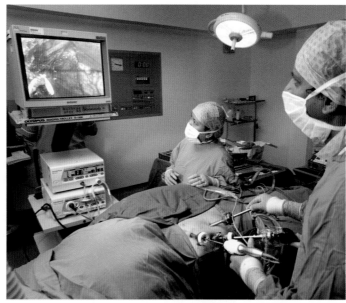

Figure B: Endoscopes use light to see inside the body. They go into the body and need skilled operators to use them.

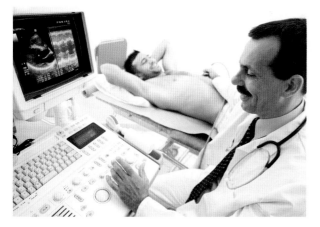

Figure C: Ultrasound scanners use sound. They are quick, cheap and simple to use but the scans can be difficult to interpret.

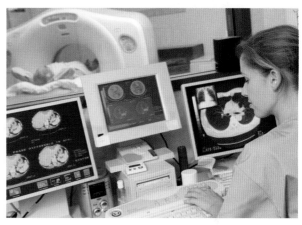

Figure D: CT scanners are big, expensive machines that use X-rays. X-rays can be dangerous in large quantities so the operator needs to be shielded from the machine

QUESTIONS

Level Booster

★★★ evaluate the benefits, drawbacks and implications of scientific developments

★★ explain the benefits, drawbacks and implications of a scientific development

★ identify benefits, drawbacks and implications of scientific developments

1 ★ Identify a benefit, a drawback and an implication of using wind turbines to generate electricity.

2 Some ways in which doctors can look inside patients are shown in the photos.

a ★★ Explain one benefit, one drawback and one implication of each of these methods.

b ★★★ Suggest two criteria that a hospital would use when trying to decide whether or not to install a CT machine. Your criteria should be able to be used to judge benefits, drawbacks and implications.

Links

Learn about decisions and risks ▶▶ **S45**

All scientific developments can create new **hazards**. A hazard is a possible source of danger or harm. A **risk** is the *chance* of harm occurring from a hazard. When people need to decide whether or not to use something new they need information about the hazards and how the risks of those hazards causing harm can be reduced.

For example, if a gas central heating system is installed in a home, the people living there need to know about the hazards of the system. One hazard of gas boilers is that they can produce a poisonous gas called carbon monoxide. The risk of this poisoning people in the home is greatly reduced if the boiler is serviced each year.

Figure A: The boiler in a gas central heating system.

Figure B: Hazards and risks.

QUESTIONS

Level Booster

★★★ treat different items differently, depending on the risk

★★ explain why some ways of controlling risk are better than others

★ recognise hazards and risks

1 a ★ List all the hazards shown in Figure B.
  b ★ Suggest one way of reducing the risk of harm from each hazard.

2 a ★★ Natural gas is burnt in a gas boiler to heat water. One hazard is that the boiler unit gets very hot. You could reduce the risk of someone burning their hand on it by putting a screen in front of it or by putting up a sign reading 'Do not touch.' Which would be better at reducing the risks? Explain your answer.
  b ★★ The exclamation mark symbol on the bottle in Figure B means 'harmful'. This symbol is used all over the world. Why is it better than just having the word 'harmful'?

3 ★★★ Why do people usually serve hot drinks in cups and not glasses? Give your answer in terms of hazards and risks.

Links

Learn about samples ▶▶ **S12**
Learn about hazards and risks ▶▶ **S24**

S46 DECISIONS ABOUT SCIENCE

Science is behind all the technology that we use. When deciding whether or not to introduce a new technology, people must consider the things that might happen (implications) – both good and bad. This includes:

* the financial cost
* the cost to the environment
* the effect on people (both individuals and different groups)
* ethics and morals (see below).

Morals are principles, **opinions** or beliefs that a person lives by. **Ethics** are what a group of people agree is right or wrong (e.g. stealing is wrong). People may disagree about ethical issues (e.g. experiments on human embryos). Often an ethical decision is based on whatever leads to the best outcome for the largest number of people.

There are laws that control certain types of scientific research so that it does not cause harm. However, other factors also influence scientific research, such as what people want (e.g. faster internet connections), politics (e.g. developing nuclear weapons) and religion (e.g. the banning of scientific books).

> Can we be sure the phones are not made using child labour?
>
> How will we dispose of the phones when they are old?
>
> Does the phone have the right functions for everyone in the company?
>
> How much will it cost the company?

Figure A: People must consider the implications of introducing new technology.

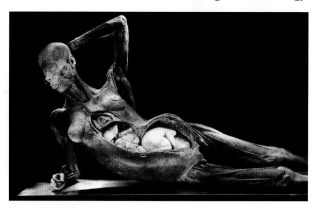

Figure B: The *Body Worlds* Exhibition.

QUESTIONS

Level Booster

★★★ explain how outside factors affect the progress and development of science

★★ describe how controversy can arise over decisions about science

★ identify influences on scientific research and new technologies

1 ★ Match each bullet point at the top of the page with one person in Figure A.

2 The *Body Worlds* Exhibition shown in Figure B is a display of real human bodies that have been treated with plastic to preserve them. People donated their bodies to this display.

a ★★ Suggest a reason why someone might be against this exhibition.

b ★★ Suggest why the exhibition was allowed to go on display.

3 ★★★ Suggest two reasons why so much scientific research has gone into making computer processors that are faster and use less power.

Links

Learn about hazards and risks ▶▶ **S24**
Learn about risk and decisions ▶▶ **S45**

QWC Science is reported and commented on by many individuals and organisations in different **media** such as TV, newspapers and the internet. You can evaluate an article using these points.

* Meaning – it is clear in its meaning?
* Up-to-date – is the information current?
* Grammar and spelling
* Good quality data (S22)
* Evidence for claims – is there evidence for the claims and opinions given? You should look out for **bias** too, such as using only a certain selection of the available evidence.
* Reveals sources of information – are they all listed?
* Sides of a debate – is the article balanced and are alternative views given?

QWC In some parts of the media, such as advertising, people try to persuade you to think in a certain way. This can be done by only giving you *some* of the evidence, but language is also important. Examples of persuasive language use include:

* using an **argument** (S41)
* repeating evidence or repeating a particular point
* using emotive language – e.g. powerful adjectives
* using the pronoun 'we' to make you feel part of something
* asking questions that encourage you to agree with a point
* using terms such as 'of course', 'it goes without saying', 'undoubtedly'.

Newspapers, magazine articles and blogs can also use persuasive language. This is particularly true if they want to influence the way someone votes in an election or if they want you to support a campaign.

Figure A: In a leaflet, the British Chiropractic Association stated that there was evidence to show that chiropractic care helps children with a range of conditions, including asthma. Chiropractic treatments involve moving joints in the spine. In an article, Simon Singh questioned the evidence used to support the BCA's opinion. Instead of debating the evidence, the BCA took him to court – but dropped the case two years later.

Figure B: Adverts use persuasive language.

Killer bugs still infest hospitals

New figures out today show Britain's hospitals are still potential death-traps.

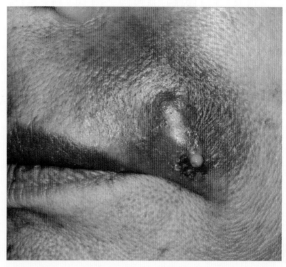

Infections with MRSA are difficult to treat and can kill.

Despite government campaigns to reduce the number of patients put at risk in our hospitals by the killer MRSA superbug, the infection rate is increasing in many hospitals. This puts patients' lives at risk. The latest figures for 162 NHS Trusts (*Health Protection Agency: Quarterly counts of MRSA bacteraemia (April 2007–March 2011)*) make for grim reading. For example, in Dartford and Gravesham there was a 400 % increase in the number of MRSA infections at the beginning of 2011 compared with the same period in 2008.

These shocking statistics show the risks patients take. How can we take this government seriously on health? These figures are a further example of this governments broken promises.

Figure C: Newspaper articles can use persuasive language.

QUESTIONS

Level Booster

- ★★★ evaluate an article using criteria and spot bias
- ★★ spot ways in which a writer tries to persuade a reader
- ★ get information from a wide range of sources

Read the article above about MRSA, which is a bacterium that can be dangerous and is difficult to kill.

1 a QWC ★ How does the writer of the article want you to feel about hospitals and MRSA?

b ★ How does the writer of the article want you to feel about the government?

c ★ Write a one-sentence summary of the article.

d ★★ How does the writer of the article try to persuade you? Give two examples.

e ★★★ Evaluate the article.

2 QWC ★ Read the advert in Figure B and identify any uses of persuasive language.

3 a QWC ★ In Simon Singh's article, what was his opinion?

b ★★★ Suggest why the BCA took Simon Singh to court.

c ★★★ Suggest why the BCA dropped their case.

Links

Learn about good quality data ▶▶ **S22**
Learn about arguments ▶▶ **S41**
Learn how scientists' papers are checked ▶▶ **S43**
Learn about synthesising ideas ▶▶ **S48**
Learn about note-taking ▶▶ **S49**

Scientists need to understand other scientists' ideas and form their own **opinions**. They then tell others about their opinions by presenting **arguments** in journal **papers**, in TV and radio broadcasts or in letters and articles in magazines, newspapers and the internet.

QWC When you read, watch or listen to something that contains scientific information, you should analyse the information.

* What subject is being discussed?
* How has the writer or speaker organised the information (e.g. in paragraphs, in bullet points, using diagrams)?
* What are the main points?
* What evidence supports these points?
* What conclusion is drawn?

QWC If you take notes, using the same structure for each article, you will be able to make connections – such as spotting how the same evidence has been used differently, or spotting points on which different authors agree or disagree. This will help you to form your own opinions, which you can then write about.

MRSA Progress Made

Hospitals in the UK are finally getting to grips with MRSA.

New figures show the hospitals are winning their fight against MRSA bacterium infections. The latest figures for 162 NHS Trusts *(Health Protection Agency: Quarterly counts of MRSA bacteraemia (April 2007–March 2011))* show a steady decrease of the MRSA problem. The total number of infections in the first quarter of 2008 (January to March) was 970. In nearly all of the following quarters there were less infections, with the January to March 2011 figure being 334; an overall 66% decrease.

Some NHS trusts are still having problems. For example, Leeds Teaching Hospitals NHS Trust had 21 cases of MRSA in the first quarter of 2011, which is well above target levels.

It is hoped that a system of fines will help to solve this. The Leeds Teaching Hospitals NHS Trust faces fines of about £400000 because of its number of MRSA infections.

Not everyone thinks that the fines system is a good idea. Former Health Secretary Edwina Currie said: "Personally I'd prefer that huge sum to be spent on extra staff, not on a fine." However, in Leeds the money is not taken out of funding for a hospital; the amount of the fine is the amount that now has to be spent on tackling the issue.

There are still battles to be won but the new figures show that great progress has been made and that there are systems in place to continue the improvement.

Regular, deep cleaning has helped to decrease the number of MRSA infections in recent years.

Figure A: Another article on MRSA.

Level Booster

★★★ evaluate differing sources of the same information to form opinions

★★ organise information from different sources to draw comparisons

★ get information from a wide range of sources

Read the article above and the one in Figure A on page 57 about MRSA, which is a bacterium that can be dangerous and is difficult to kill.

1 **a** ★ How many NHS Trusts are there?

b ★ From January to March 2008, Dartford and Gravesham NHS Trust had two cases of MRSA infection. How many did they have from January to March 2011?

c ★ List two main points that the writer of the article on page 57 is making.

d ★ List two main points that the writer of the article on page 58 is making.

e ★★ On what point do the two authors agree?

f ★★ How have the two authors reached different opinions, using the same data?

g ★★★ Both articles give information about an increase or decrease in infections. From which article can you obtain the best evidence for this? Explain your reasoning.

Links

Learn about arguments ▶▶ **S41**

Learn how scientists write papers ▶▶ **S43**

Learn about what makes a good article ▶▶ **S47**

QWC When you read, watch or listen to scientific information, you should make notes. Some people make notes using tables, others use headings and subheadings, and others use concept maps. Your notes do not need to be seen by anyone else – but you should be able to read them back at a later time and understand what they mean.

QWC When examining some text:
- read it through quickly first, concentrating on broadly understanding it
- read it through slowly, writing down unfamiliar words (which you may need to look up)
- write down the main ideas and points – use short, summary-style sentences and use your own words; it's pointless just copying out chunks of a text
- add arrows and symbols to link ideas together and highlight important points.

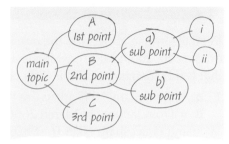

Figure A: There are many different ways of structuring your notes.

PAF

QWC When it comes to planning your own writing, think about PAF (Figure B). This will help you to think about the overall style and structure of what you are going to write. PAF stands for purpose, audience, format.

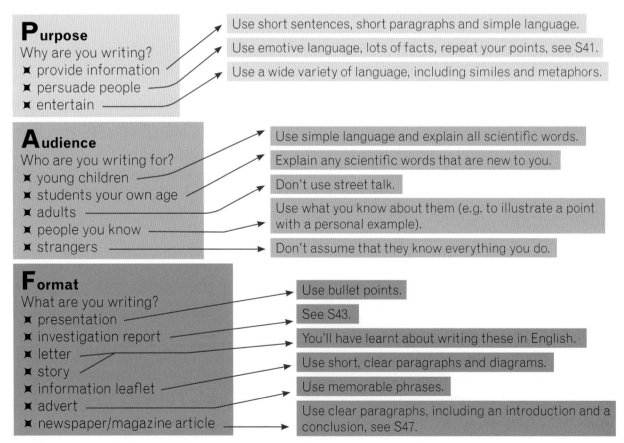

Purpose
Why are you writing?
- provide information
- persuade people
- entertain

Use short sentences, short paragraphs and simple language.

Use emotive language, lots of facts, repeat your points, see S41.

Use a wide variety of language, including similes and metaphors.

Audience
Who are you writing for?
- young children
- students your own age
- adults
- people you know
- strangers

Use simple language and explain all scientific words.

Explain any scientific words that are new to you.

Don't use street talk.

Use what you know about them (e.g. to illustrate a point with a personal example).

Don't assume that they know everything you do.

Format
What are you writing?
- presentation
- investigation report
- letter
- story
- information leaflet
- advert
- newspaper/magazine article

Use bullet points.

See S43.

You'll have learnt about writing these in English.

Use short, clear paragraphs and diagrams.

Use memorable phrases.

Use clear paragraphs, including an introduction and a conclusion, see S47.

Figure B: Think PAF when planning how to write something.

[QWC] Before you actually start writing, it's a good idea to sketch out how you are going to organise your information. If you are writing an article, you will need to use paragraphs to group your information. You could use a writing frame like this:

- headline – gives the main point of the article in a few words
- introductory paragraph – summarises the whole article
- main part of article
  - first paragraph has a main point and gives reasons or evidence to back up the point
  - second paragraph has another main point, with reasons or evidence
  - etc.
- conclusion – restates the main point of the article again.

PEA

It is often difficult to know how to structure a paragraph, either for a long answer to a question or as part of an article. You can use the PEA writing frame to help you put things in a good order. PEA stands for point, evidence, analysis. So your paragraph will make a point, and then provide some evidence or reasons to support that point. In the last part of the paragraph you explain the link between your evidence or reasons and your point. Figure C gives a couple of examples.

[QWC] Always remember to check your punctuation, spelling and grammar too!

We must do more to protect the habitat of the red panda. Scientists think that there are only a few hundred red pandas left in Nepal. Since 1990 Nepal has lost about a quarter of its woodlands. If this destruction continues the red pandas will have nowhere to live.	**Point** **Evidence** **Analysis**	The freezing point of pure water is 0 °C. When we take pure water and cool it to below 0 °C it all becomes ice. This is because when there is less heat energy in the water molecules they vibrate less and can form stronger bonds.

Figure C: Use PEA when planning paragraphs.

QUESTIONS

Level Booster

- ★★★ explain why scientific information needs to be written in different ways
- ★★ organise scientific writing to make it appropriate for different audiences
- ★ organise scientific writing into clear paragraphs and points

1 Look at the newspaper report in Figure A on page 58 in S48.

  a **[QWC]** ★ In the paragraph starting 'New figures show …' identify the point, the evidence and the explanation.

  b **[QWC]** ★ Make notes on this article.

  c **[QWC]** ★★ How would you change the article to be read by young children?

  d **[QWC]** ★★ Rewrite the article for young children, concentrating on only the main points.

2 ★★★ Why is it important to write about science in different ways? Make two main points in your answer.

Links

Learn about analysing and synthesising ▶▶ **S48**

COMMAND WORDS

QWC Words that tell you how to answer a question are called command words (or imperatives). It's important that you know what they mean. The table will help you.

Command	Notes
Assess	See 'Evaluate' below.
Calculate	Work out an answer, using numbers. Always show your working. Always put in the units.
Compare	Describe the differences/similarities between things, or their advantages/drawbacks. It's a good idea to plan this by drawing a table. You can then use this writing frame: • write down something about each different thing • point out the similarities/differences.
Complete	Fill in answers in a space or finish writing a sentence.
Define	State briefly what something means.
Describe	Recall facts in an accurate way or say what a diagram or graph shows – e.g. what trend you can see.
Discuss	Build up an argument about an issue. Use the writing frame in S41.
Estimate	Make a rough calculation.
Evaluate Also: Assess	Say how good or poor something is, based on a series of points. If you are asked to evaluate more than one thing then you need to compare the things and then state which is best, with reasons. You could use this writing frame: • write down something about each different thing • point out the similarities/differences • state which is best • give reasons for your choice.
Explain	State the reasons why something happens. You must explain the links between your reasons and what you are explaining – don't just write down a list of reasons. Think about using the PEA writing frame in S49.
Give	See 'write down' below.
Identify	Look at some data or text and pick out a certain part.
Illustrate	Give examples in an explanation or description. A good way to do this is to explain/describe something and then use the words 'for example' to introduce an example.
Justify	Evaluate (see above) but also give valid evidence for your choice of which is best, rather than just giving some reasons.
List	Write down key points in a brief way.
Name	See 'write down' below.
Outline Also: Summarise	State the main points of an argument or of how something happens. This can be done in a list of bullet points.

Command	Notes
State	See 'Write down' below.
Suggest	Use your scientific knowledge to work out what is happening in an unfamiliar situation.
Summarise	See 'outline' above.
Use the information	Use the information given to answer the question. You won't get any marks unless you use the information given.
Write down Also: Give, Name, State	State a fact or give an example. If a question asks for two examples (or has 2 marks) only write down two. Otherwise, you risk writing something that is incorrect and losing marks.

Throughout history there have been stories about animals behaving in odd ways just before an earthquake happens.

In 2009, some scientists were watching the breeding of some common toads around a lake in Italy. Normally, once breeding has started towards the end of March, the toads stay at the site in large numbers for between 3 and 7 weeks. However, the scientists noticed something strange happening to the number of toads at the start of April and this was followed by an earthquake. The tables below show the number of male toads seen by the scientists around the lake each day during the study.

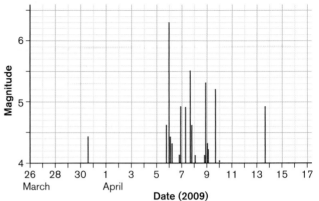

Figure A: The strength (magnitude) of the rock movements during the earthquake in April 2009 and the foreshocks and aftershocks (less powerful rock movements before and after an earthquake).

Date	Number of male toads
26/3	18
27/3	91
28/3	88
29/3	80
30/3	9
31/3	2

Date	Number of male toads
01/4	1
02/4	1
03/4	1
04/4	2
05/4	0
06/4	3

Date	Number of male toads
07/4	19
08/4	35
09/4	10
10/4	8
11/4	3
12/4	5

Date	Number of male toads
13/4	3
14/4	5
15/4	3
16/4	40
17/4	44

QUESTIONS

1 ▶▶ **S30** What was strange about the number of toads at the beginning of April?

2 ▶▶ **S33** Plot the data in the table as a line graph.

3 ▶▶ **S31** On what date did the earthquake strike?

4 ▶▶ **S2** Suggest a question that the scientists asked themselves after the earthquake.

5 ▶▶ **S3** The scientists think that the huge forces on the underground rocks just before an earthquake cause chemical reactions that make water more acidic.
   a What is an idea like this called?
   b Write down one prediction that could be made from this idea.

6 ▶▶ **S20** What is the range of the number of toads in the tables?

7 The scientists who collected the data on the toads then worked with some other scientists to help them with their ideas. Together, they published a paper in 2011.
   a ▶▶ **S25** Did their paper use primary or secondary evidence? Explain your answer.
   b ▶▶ **S43** Outline the process that the paper went through before being published.

8 ▶▶ **S27** What was the percentage decrease in male toad numbers between 29 March and 30 March?

CRUMBLING MATERIALS

To make buildings that can withstand the pollution in our big cities, scientists experiment with different building materials in laboratories to find out which materials are best. In an experiment, two types of similar stone were put in containers of air mixed with different amounts of sulfur dioxide. After a year, the masses of the rock samples were measured and the percentage decrease in mass was calculated for each. The results are shown in the table.

Figure A: The Taj Mahal has been badly damaged by sulfur dioxide.

Mass of sulfur dioxide reaching the surface of the rock each day (mg/m²)		10	20	30	40	50	60	70	80	90	100
Loss in mass during the year (%)	Rock 1	1.00	1.10	1.30	1.40	1.50	1.90	1.80	1.90	2.10	2.20
	Rock 2	1.10	1.20	1.40	1.60	1.70	2.00	2.20	2.50	2.60	2.90

QUESTIONS

1 a ▶▶ **S5** Is the data in the table qualitative or quantitative?
   b Is the data continuous or discrete?

2 a ▶▶ **S13** What were the dependent and the independent variables in this investigation?
   b Give two of the control variables that should be considered.

3 ▶▶ **S38** Plot the data on an appropriate chart or graph.

4 ▶▶ **S19** Which point on the graph is anomalous?

5 a ▶▶ **S6, S9** What unit is the mass of the sulfur dioxide reaching the rock surface measured in? Write out the name in words.

   b What is a unit that is made up of two other units called?
   c ▶▶ **S26** Why do scientists use symbols for units? Give two reasons.

6 ▶▶ **S8** Each piece of rock measured 1.5 cm by 4 cm by 4 cm. Calculate the surface area of each piece of rock.

7 ▶▶ **S24** Suggest one hazard and a way of reducing the risk in this investigation.

8 ▶▶ **S42** Suggest one way in which the investigation could be improved.

9 ▶▶ **S15** What correlation is there in the results?

BIMETALLIC STRIPS

A bimetallic strip is a made of two strips of different metals joined together along their entire length, one on top of the other. They are used in clocks, thermometers, thermostats and circuit breakers.

All metals expand when they are heated and contract when they are cooled. This is because the particles (atoms) that make up metals need more space to move around at higher temperatures. When two different metals are stuck to one another in a strip, the strip will bend if heated or cooled. This is because different metals expand and contract by different amounts when heated and cooled.

In an experiment, some scientists wanted to find out if some common, pure metals expanded by different amounts when heated. Bars of seven metals 25 cm long at 20°C were heated to 40°C. The changes in length were measured in three tests.

Figure A: The coils in the back of thermometers like this are a bimetallic strip. They are curled tighter or more loosely depending on the temperature.

Metal	Increase in length of 25 cm bar (µm)*		
	Test 1	Test 2	Test 3
aluminium	120	119	121
copper	86	84	83
gold	71	70	70
iron	65	57	59
nickel	66	64	63
titanium	43	42	44
tungsten	25	21	22

*1000 µm = 1 mm.

QUESTIONS

1 ▶▶ **S18** To how many significant figures is the data for aluminium given?

2 a ▶▶ **S20** Calculate mean readings for each metal.
   b What is the point of calculating means?
   c ▶▶ **S38** Plot your means on an appropriate chart or graph.

3 ▶▶ **S6, S7** Convert the lengths measured in Test 1 to millimetres.

4 a ▶▶ **S40** Using circles to represent particles (atoms), draw a model to represent what happens inside a metal when it is heated.
   b Why do scientists use models?

5 ▶▶ **S39** Which combination of metals from the table would produce the most bending in a bimetallic strip? Explain your reasoning.

6 ▶▶ **S16** For which metal are the results the most precise?

7 ▶▶ **S42** [QWC] Evaluate the results in the table.

8 ▶▶ **S49** [QWC] Use information on this page to rewrite the second paragraph (above) as two paragraphs, each with a point, a piece of evidence and an explanation.

Answers

S1 THE SCIENTIFIC METHOD

1 a A statement saying what you think will happen in an experiment.

b So that you can see if an idea is correct.

2 a No

b The idea is wrong. If the idea were correct then only the plants near the window with plants outside it would have bent.

3

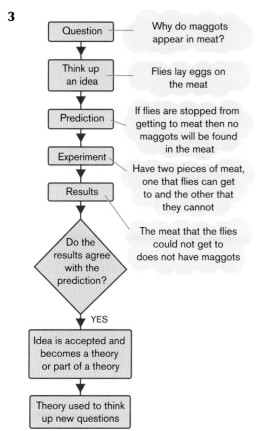

Note that there is not a 'no' line going back to the 'idea' box because Redi's experiment results agreed with his prediction.

S2 SCIENTIFIC QUESTIONS

1 a Should I paint my bathroom that nice blue colour?

b It is not a question that can be answered by doing an experiment.

2 a We haven't done enough experiments on this yet. It is quite possible to work out the code for a giraffe and it will be done in the future, but scientists have not got around to it yet.

b The experiments are too expensive. It will involve sending a spacecraft to *Callisto* to drill down into its surface. *You could also say that not enough experiments have been done yet although maybe it will become cheaper (or more important) to do this exploration in the future.*

3 a Which is more fizzy, Pepsi or Coke? What gives wine gums their taste? Why do skis slide on snow? *Remember that anything that can't be shown to be incorrect or correct by doing experiments is not a scientific question. Things like 'finding cricket boring' are just opinions.*

b Two points from: they can be answered by doing experiments, they can be used to think up ideas about how or why things happens, they can be answered by making observations/ measurements, when answered they can be used to make up new questions.

S3 HYPOTHESES AND PREDICTIONS

1 **QWC** *If* I look at any cell using a microscope *then* I will be able to find a nucleus. *Your answer doesn't need to be exactly like this – just along those lines. Although you don't have to use 'if … then …' it's a very useful habit to get into and will really help you think about what a prediction is.*

2 **QWC** A hypothesis. It is a scientific idea about why something happens OR it is not a statement of what will happen if something changes. *Remember, a scientific idea (or hypothesis) is a statement that <u>explains why</u> something might happen but a prediction is a statement that <u>describes what</u> will happen if something is changed.*

3 a **QWC** If I eat more chocolate <u>then</u> I will get more spots. *Don't worry, there is no evidence that chocolate causes spots!*

b **QWC** If I add more salt to some water <u>then</u> its boiling point will go up/go down/change.

4 The longer you heat some water the hotter it gets OR if you heat a pan of water/put on the kettle it eventually boils. *There are other answers but these are the sorts of additional pieces of information that could have been used when putting the hypothesis together.*

5 a Scientists connect together existing pieces of information in new ways.

b A hypothesis is judged using evidence from experiments, which are planned using a strict set of rules. A fiction plot is judged by what a range of people think. There are no strict rules to say what is right and what is wrong with a fiction plot. *We describe the way hypotheses are looked at as being 'objective', which means that the decision is not based on personal feelings, tastes or opinions. The way in which a fiction plot is judged is 'subjective', which means that the decision is based on personal feelings, tastes and opinions.*

S4 THEORIES

1 a They need to collect results that they can use as evidence to support or disprove an idea.

b The results of an experiment agree with the predictions made by the idea.

2 It is not a theory. *It is only a guess and cannot be tested.*

3 A theory can contain many hypotheses, each of which contains evidence to support it. And so there is a lot of evidence to support a whole theory. *All theories develop and change over time. As time goes on scientists modify them.*

4 *It doesn't matter which of the three hypotheses in the drawing you choose, but you should include the following points:*

- a prediction is made
- the prediction is tested in an experiment
- the results from the experiment are used as evidence
- if the results agree with the prediction, the results are evidence that supports the hypothesis
- if the results disagree with the prediction, the results are evidence that disproves the hypothesis (or even the whole theory).

S5 QUALITATIVE DATA AND QUANTITATIVE DATA

1 a categoric/qualitative;

b quantitative and discrete;

c quantitative and continuous

2 25 mm, 60%, 0.089 cm³. *Remember that a value has to be a number and it also has to have something saying what that number means.*

3 a Categoric/qualitative (the names of the teams) and quantitative discrete (the points that they scored).

b Ordering the qualitative data alphabetically:

Team A – 2 points, Team B – 5 points, Team C – 7 points, Team D – 3 points

Ordering the quantitative data in decreasing number order:

Team C – 7 points, Team B – 5 points, D – 3 points, Team A – 2 points

Ordering the quantitative data in increasing number order:

Team A – 2 points, Team D – 3 points, Team B – 5 points, Team C – 7 points

You could also order the data in reverse alphabetical order but that isn't a very common way of ordering information.

4 You could collect qualitative data – feeling how warm the tubes get. You could collect quantitative data with a thermometer and record by how much the temperature increased.

S6 THE SI SYSTEM

1 a metre; **b** degrees Celsius *Note that Celsius has a capital C*; **c** kilograms; **d** millimetres; **e** micrograms; **f** kilohertz; **g** megawatts; **h** millivolts; **i** decimetres; **j** centiseconds.

2 a 10 mm *There are 1000 millimetres in a metre. There are 100 centimetres in a metre. So the number of millimetres is ten times bigger than the number of centimetres. Don't forget the units!*

b 10 000 mm *There are 1000 millimetres in a metre. So 10 × 1000 = 10 000 mm*

c 10 mm *Trick question!*

d 0.1 mm *There are 1 000 000 micrometres in a metre. There are 1000 millimetres in a metre. 1 000 000 ÷ 1000 = 1000 so the number of millimetres is 1000 times less than the number of micrometres. 100 ÷ 1000 = 0.1 mm*

3 To make communication easier. *There are other answers to this. As long as you've got the idea* *that it makes sharing ideas between scientists easier then you have the right idea.*

4 a Kilometres/km. *Note that the question wants you to use SI units; 'mile' is not an SI unit.*

  b Milligrams/mg or micrograms/µg. *The average mass of a 12 cm long human hair is about 0.62 mg or 620 µg.*

  c Milliseconds/ms or microseconds/µs *Some of the fastest cameras will be able to keep their shutters open for just $\frac{1}{8000}$ of second, which is 0.125 milliseconds or 125 µs.*

  d Volts/V or kilovolts/kV *The voltage is about 400 000 V or 400 kV. Make sure you write kV with a lower case 'k' and a capital 'V'.*

S7 INDEX FORM AND INTERCONVERSIONS

Don't forget the units!

1 a metres cubed; **b** kilometres squared; **c** five squared; **d** eight squared; **e** nine cubed

2 It saves time and it is recognised by scientists all over the world.

3 a $10 \times 5 \times 6 = 300 \, cm^3$

  b Two of $10 \times 5 = 50 \, cm^2$; two of $5 \times 6 = 30 \, cm^2$; two of $10 \times 6 = 60 \, cm^2$

4 1 km is 1000 m; so the field is $1000 \times 55 = 55\,000 \, m^2$

5 $1 \, m^3 = 10 \times 10 \times 10 = 1000 \, dm^3$. The pool is $5 \times 5 \times 2 = 50 \, m^3$, which is $50 \times 1000 = 50\,000 \, dm^3$. *You could have used the conversion factor of 10 dm in each metre for each side of the pool. So the pool is $(10 \times 5) \times (10 \times 5) \times (10 \times 2) = 50 \times 50 \times 20 = 50\,000 \, dm^3$.*

S8 CALCULATING PERIMETERS, AREAS AND VOLUMES

Don't forget the units!

1 a Measuring tape. *A fairly long one!*

  b $100 + 100 + 75 + 75 = 350 \, m$

  c $100 \times 75 = 7500 \, m^2$

2 $0.5 \times 0.5 = 0.25 \, m^2$

3 a Surface area $= 2(4 \times 6) + 2(4 \times 10) + 2(6 \times 10) = 48 + 80 + 120 = 248 \, cm^2$

  b Volume $= 4 \times 6 \times 10 = 240 \, cm^3$

4 a Cuboid surface area $= 2(2 \times 0.2) + 2(2 \times 1.5) + 2(0.2 \times 1.5) = 0.8 + 6.0 + 0.6 = 7.4 \, cm^2$

  Cube surface area $= 2(1 \times 1) + 2(1 \times 1) + 2(1 \times 1) = 2 + 2 + 2 = 6 \, cm^2$

  So the cuboid has the greater surface area.

  b Cuboid volume $= 2 \times 0.2 \times 1.5 = 0.6 \, cm^3$; cube volume $= 1 \times 1 \times 1 = 1 \, cm^3$

  So the cube has the greater volume.

5 a $1.5 + 2 + 4 = 7.5 \, cm$

  b The height of the triangle.

6 a Circumference $= 2\pi r = 2 \times 3.14 \times 4.5 = 28.26 \, cm$. *Remember that the radius of a circle is half its diameter.*

  b Area $= \pi r^2 = 3.14 \times 4.5^2 = 3.14 \times (4.5 \times 4.5) = 63.59 \, cm^2$

S9 COMPOUND MEASURES

1 N/cm^2, m/g, mm/°C. *All the others contain a distance unit followed by a 'per' and then a time unit, which makes them units for speed.*

2 a km, °C, m, g. *All compound units need to have two different units in them.*

  b N/cm^2 – newtons per centimetre squared or newtons per square centimetre

  cm/s – centimetres per second

  kg/m^3 – kilograms per metre cubed or kilograms per cubic metre

  V/m – volts per metre.

  Have a look at S6 if you got any of these wrong.

3 m/s or metres per second

4 cm/day or centimetres per day

5 $1.7 \, g/cm^3$

6 Steel. It has a density of $7.8 \, g/cm^3$ whereas rubber has a density of $1.5 \, g/cm^3$, which is a lower figure.

7 $0.5 \, MN/m^2$

8 J/s or joules per second

S10 MANAGING LARGE NUMBERS

1 a 8; **b** 3; **c** 7

2 a Ninety eight thousand six hundred and twenty four

b Six million eight hundred and forty five thousand seven hundred and nine

3 a 98 624; **b** 6 845 709

4 It's a power of 10 and means 10 multiplied by itself six times (seven 'lots' of 10 multiplied together).

5 a 2 000 000. *You should include gaps between groups of three digits.*

b 86 500; **c** 108 967.8

S11 ESTIMATES: ROUNDING AND SAMPLES

1 a i 5690; **ii** 2440; **iii** 7560; **iv** 56 070; **v** 235 690

b i 5700; **ii** 2400; **iii** 7600; **iv** 56 100; **v** 235 700

c i 6000; **ii** 2000; **iii** 8000; **iv** 56 000; **v** 236 000

2 3 790 000

3 a Spots in sample: 3

Sample area: $2 \times 2 \, cm^2 = 4 \, cm^2$, whole area: $6 \times 6 \, cm^2 = 36 \, cm^2$

Whole area compared with sample: $36 \div 4 = 9$

Estimate of total number of spots: $9 \times 3 = 27$

b Spots in sample: 3; estimate of total number of spots: $9 \times 3 = 27$

c Spots in sample: 8; estimate of total number of spots: $9 \times 8 = 72$

d Use a larger sample size.

4 The pitches are only likely to vary by metres and not tens of metres; so his estimate will not be good enough (detailed enough) to give him an answer.

S12 SAMPLES AND BIAS

1 a Up; **b** Left

c The gun was not set correctly or the person was aiming at the wrong part of the target.

2 She did not use enough samples.

3 a To make others think that his team is better than it really is.

b It is using evidence that is shifted away from its true value.

4 She needs to use enough samples; and she must choose where to take the samples randomly.

You need to mention both of these points.

S13 VARIABLES AND FAIR TESTS

1 Independent variable – amounts of salt; Dependent variable – boiling point;

Control variables – volume of water, same heating apparatus, same thermometer.

There are other control variables that could be included that are not mentioned in the description. For example, type of salt, type of water.

2 a i Independent variable – amount of light; Dependent variable – number of maggots; Control variables – moisture, colour of light, type (species) of maggots.

ii Independent variable – type of antacid; Dependent variable – change in acidity/alkalinity/pH; Control variables – amount of antacid, type/strength/concentration of acid, amount of acid, way of measuring acidity/alkalinity/pH.

iii Independent variable – size of magnet; Dependent variable – number of paper clips picked up; Control variables – type of paper clips, size/mass of paper clips, type of magnet.

b *You only need one of these for each of the three investigations.*

i *Moisture:* an area with brighter light may cause that area to be drier than an area with dimmer light. If this happens you are not doing a fair test because it's not only the independent variable that is changing. Maggots may prefer damper areas to drier ones no matter what the light levels are.

Colour of light: if you use different bulbs for different light intensities, you may find that they are different colours. Again, this would mean that you are not doing a fair test and maggots might prefer one colour of light over another with the actual amount of light not being so important.

Species of maggots: if you use different species of maggots in the test, it may be that one species prefers lighter areas than another.

ii *Amount of antacid:* if you just put different antacid tablets into the acids, you may find that the different tablets contain different amounts of antacid ingredient, so the ones with a greater quantity of a less good antacid may seem to work better.

Type/strength/concentration of acid: the type of acid may affect how well an antacid works. This might mean that a poor antacid may seem to work better but only because it is in an acid that reacts well with antacids.

Amount of acid: if you just put antacids into different amounts of acid, you may find that a less good antacid seems to work better but only because it is in less acid.

Way of measuring acidity/alkalinity/pH: if you don't measure something in the same way each time you cannot compare measurements, because you cannot be sure that the apparatus is measuring exactly the same thing in exactly the same way.

iii *Type of paper clips:* paper clips made of a different material may be attracted more or less to the same magnet, so you would not just be measuring the 'strength' of the magnet.

Size/mass of paper clips: paper clips of a different mass may be attracted more or less to the same magnet, so you would not just be measuring the 'strength' of the magnet.

Type of magnet: magnets made of different materials may not be as strong as each other. If you used different kinds of magnets you would not do a fair test because it's not only the independent variable that is changing.

S14 CONTROLS

1 C and D; *these two both use organisms and there are too many control variables when it comes to doing investigations with organisms.*

2 A control experiment includes a part where the independent variable is not used.

3 a The control would be to have a circuit with no cells. *The independent variable is the number of cells and so removing it would mean removing all the cells.*

b No. There are only a few control variables in this experiment and they are easy to control so you would not include a control.

4 • A set of people would be selected and divided

into groups.
- The groups should contain similar people so that the drugs will work the same way in the different groups.
- People in one group would take the new drug when they had a headache, and people in the other groups would take standard headache drugs.
- A final group would be a control and people in it would not take the drug. The control allows the scientists to make sure that it is the drug that is helping to get rid of the headache and not something else.

There are two parts that you need to have in your answer – having similar groups and using a control group. The question also asks you to 'explain' and so you need to explain the importance of these two things. Note that in a drug test like this, the people in the control group would probably be given what's called a 'placebo'. This is something that looks like a headache pill but contains no actual drug.

S15 RELATIONSHIPS

1 If a woman has hCG in her urine she is pregnant.

2 The older the boy, the faster he is.

3 a A; **b** C and D; **c** B

*In part **b**, just because the graph is going 'down' in D does not mean that there is no relationship – the relationship is just going the other way. It still shows that a steady change in the independent variable is matched by a steady change in the dependent variable.*

4 Because the points all stick close to the main pattern/trend. *This is an example of a strong relationship and strong relationships are more likely to be caused by an independent variable having a direct affect on a dependent variable.*

5 It makes it much easier to spot patterns because you can see what happens to all the data in one glance, rather than having to compare the actual numbers.

S16 ACCURACY AND PRECISION

1 a 15.9 cm in the first set of measurements, and 17.0 in the second set. This is because these readings are the ones closest to the real values.

b 16.2 cm *It is the one that is furthest away from the real value.*

2 You may not be able to draw a conclusion from a set of results. *A conclusion is what you have managed to work out about a scientific question from some data. If your data is not very accurate then you won't be able to use it to answer the question.*

3 a Her readings for the real value of 16.0 cm are more precise because the readings are more closely grouped together.

b If readings are closely grouped together then you can be more sure that the readings are correct.

4 Yes. All her measurements can be divided into two clear groups, with the heights of one group all being higher than the heights in the other group. There are no measurements that are very far away from all the others. *If there were an overlap between the two sets of readings there would have been more of a problem and you would need to take some more readings.*

S17 ERRORS IN MEASUREMENTS

1 Mistakes in results made by people not doing things correctly.

2 a The results for group B contain more errors because the differences between the readings are greater. *If you have looked at S16 you might have talked about how the results from group B are less precise than those for group A.*

b If the results contain many errors you cannot be sure which is correct.

c The acid may not have been measured out accurately using a measuring cylinder; someone might have not read the scale from the correct angle. Also the masses may not have been measured properly; group B's balance may have been faulty; it may not have been set to zero before each measurement.

3 a 21 cm^3

b You should be level with the part of the scale that you need to read.

c 21.1 cm^3 *Remember that you read a scale at its edge – where the top red dashed line crosses out of the cylinder into the air.*

4 *There are a number of improvements that could be made. Note that you are asked to* explain *the improvements, not just state what they are. Good examples are:*

- Make sure that only one person reads the scale on the measuring cylinder and that they do this by being level with the scale. This is so that the readings from the scale will all be made in the same way and therefore be more accurate.
- Make sure that the balance is set to zero before any copper oxide is added. This will make sure that the readings are more accurate and precise.

S18 SIGNIFICANT FIGURES

1 a 62 796; **b** 70 000

2 a 5300; **b** 2900; **c** 17 200 *If you have got these wrong, look at S11.*

3 More accurate figures take longer to sort out and divide into groups (they are more complicated to work with) and the year groups can easily be worked out using less accurate numbers.

4 20 cm^3 divisions. *A litre (1000 cm^3) measuring cylinder is often marked up in 20 cm^3 divisions. You would only need to use a measuring cylinder with 1 cm^3 divisions if you were asked to measure out some water to a much greater degree of accuracy (e.g. 1001 cm^3). 1000 cm^3 is only to one significant figure and so you do not need that much accuracy in the measuring cylinder.*

5 Matilda's starting mass is to 2 significant figures; the hair is to 1 significant figure. Her mass minus the hair is given to 6 significant figures! *Don't get confused with 'decimal places'. The number of 'decimal places' that a value has is the number of digits after the decimal point. The number of significant figures ignores the decimal point and tells you the number of digits that show something's value.*

6 a 289 687 to 2 significant figures = 290 000; 0.003 452 3 to 2 significant figures = 0.0035

b 289 687 to 4 significant figures = 289 700; 0.003 452 3 to 4 significant figures = 0.003 452

7 62 × 5.1 = 320 m (to 2 significant figures). *Hope you haven't written 316.2! This is to 4 significant figures – but the starting figures each only had 2 significant figures. When doing calculations, do* *not give your answer to more significant figures than the least accurate value that you started with.*

S19 ANOMALOUS RESULTS AND OUTLIERS

1 They are the results that don't fit the same pattern as the other results.

2 The point at 2 V (the third point from the left).

3 a 18.9 s at 20°C and 1.3 s at 57°C. These are very different from the other two readings at the same temperature. *Make sure you are clear in answering this question and you have not just said '1.3 s' – there are two readings at 1.3 s but only one of them is an anomaly.*

b One from:
- stopping/starting the stop watch too early/late
- getting the temperatures of the syrups mixed up
- not copying the time from the stop watch correctly.

Whatever you wrote in your answer, make sure you can see why each of the ways listed here would cause an anomalous result.

c Leave them out when calculating means.

4 For all of these, one way of making sure that anomalous results don't affect your results is to do lots of repeat readings, and then ignore any readings that don't match the others. Other possible causes of anomalous results and ways to avoid them are:
- not counting the bubbles properly – use a clicker to count the bubbles rather than counting them in your head and risk losing count
- not timing one minute accurately enough – use a countdown timer, which bleeps after 1 minute to tell you to stop timing
- getting the water temperatures mixed up – clearly label the temperature on each container of water
- not using the same amount of pond weed – use a balance to measure out the same mass of pond weed for each part of the investigation
- not using the same species of pond weed – use pond weed from only one source.

5 For all of these, one way of making sure that anomalous results don't affect your results is to do lots of repeat readings, and then ignore any readings that don't match the others. Possible causes of anomalous results and ways to avoid them are:
- not measuring out 15 cm³ of liquid each time – make sure that a measuring device with enough accuracy is used (e.g. a measuring cylinder with divisions of 1 cm³)
- make sure that the scale is read properly, with the person looking at the scale being level with it
- it's also a good idea for the same person to read the scale each time because this avoids errors caused by different people looking at the scale in slightly different ways.
- not measuring out the solid to enough accuracy – use a balance that is accurate to 0.1 g
- make sure that the balance is set to zero each time before you use it
- not reading the temperature on the thermometer properly – see the suggestions above about reading from a scale.

S20 MEANS AND RANGES

1 82.7 − 24.0 = 58.7 s *Did you forget the units? A range is the difference between the top and bottom values, so you need to subtract one from the other. It's often helpful to put in what those top and bottom values were and write out the sum in full.*

2 a 27.1 − 24.3 = 2.8°C

b For Mike's readings: 27 + 28 + 38 + 23 + 22 = 138

$\frac{138}{5} = 28°C$.

Did you write 27.6°C? That's OK but remember that you really should give your answer to the same number of significant figures as the original data. If you're not sure about this have a look at S18.

For Jasmin's readings: 25.1 + 24.3 + 25.2 + 26.3 + 27.0 + 27.1 = 155

$\frac{155}{6} = 25.8°C$

Make sure that you divided by 6 here because Jasmin took 6 readings whereas Mike only took 5. And again, you really should use the same number of significant figures as the original data.

c Jasmin's because her repeated readings show a narrower range.

3 They may make the range much bigger than it really should be.

4 a $\frac{204.7}{6}$ = 34.1 s *Don't forget the units!*

b One or two very wrong readings can have a large effect on a mean making it very inaccurate.

c Sometimes it's difficult to judge whether a result is anomalous or not and you may then ignore a result that is actually important.

S21 VALIDITY

1 • Independent variable: change the material covering the cup.
 • Dependent variable: measure the temperature of the liquid after a set amount of time.
 • Control variables: the amount of liquid, the type of liquid, the size of cup, the shape of cup, the material that the cup is made from, the thermometer used to make the measurements, the time that the cup is left to cool.

2 a Yes. His prediction links the length of the resistance wire to the current. His results table shows that he has changed the length of the wire and measured the current.

b The results are not valid because they are not repeatable. *According to his table, the results show the current using different lengths of the wire, but because they are not repeatable there must be something wrong and they are not valid. He would need to check his method and his apparatus. For example, he might not have connected the ammeter properly or the ammeter may be faulty.*

c The results do not match the predictions.

3 The investigation is not valid because the results do not let you answer the original question, which was about the number of bacteria and not the number of different types of bacteria. *Note the word 'explain' in the question – you can't just answer this question with a 'yes' or a 'no'.*

S22 REPEATABILITY AND RELIABILITY

1 So that you can be more sure that your readings are correct.

2 a He did not have any repeated measurements for a particular depth. Also he does not have enough readings over a good enough range to see a pattern. *It could be just by chance that the sample KJ took from 1 m deep contained far more water fleas than normal and actually there are fewer water fleas the deeper you go. You just can't tell from this data.*

b There are three separate points you should get here:
 • take readings at more different depths
 • take readings over the whole range of the pond, down to 2 m
 • take three or four repeat measurements at each depth.

3 a The data from group A. It contains more readings than the data from group B; the readings are all repeatable; and it contains no anomalous results (group B's reading of 9.1 cm for 200 g is anomalous).

b 100 g. *Remember that precision is a measure of how close together readings are. The readings for 100 g are all very close to each other and much more so than for the other masses. If you got this wrong, have a look at S16.*

c Yes. There are many readings and the results for each different mass are repeatable, apart from one anomalous result of 9.1 cm for 200 g, which can be ignored because the rest of the results form a regular pattern. *If you're confused by the conclusion, do some rounding. The results for 100 g are about 4 cm, for 2 × 100 g the result is about 8 cm and for 2 × 200 g the result is about 16 cm. This is much easier to see if you plot the results on a graph (S33). It is also much easier to see anomalous results using a graph.*

S23 TRIAL RUNS

1 a A quick version of an investigation method.

b Two from:
 • to work out the range of measurements needed

- work out the interval needed between the measurements
- to work out how many measurements to take
- to make sure a method works
- to make sure you have the correct apparatus
- to make sure that you have measuring apparatus that is accurate enough
- to make sure that your investigation is safe.

2 a One from:

- the distance the elastic band is stretched back
- the elastic band, the distance between the two nails
- the surface over which the mass travels
- the shape of the mass.

b i The heavier the mass, the less distance it will travel.

ii 10–100 g

iii 10 g or 20 g

iv To the nearest cm or nearest mm.

c i The pattern is difficult to spot because there are only a few readings, but it looks like lighter masses move further than heavier ones – this makes sense because less energy is needed to move lighter things.

ii The range used in the trial is OK because it gives a wide range of results for the distance travelled, which can easily be measured.

iii 5 g is going to be too small an interval because there is no difference between the results for the 10 g mass and the 15 g mass. You need to have intervals that are wide apart enough to show a difference, otherwise you end up spending a lot of time measuring things for no real reason. You need enough readings to show a very clear pattern.

iv The pattern will be clear by measuring in cm or mm. *However, you can probably draw a better graph by measuring in mm.*

S24 SAFETY: RISKS AND HAZARDS

1 a One from:

- spilling alkali/acid
- acid/alkali splashing on skin/into eyes

b One from:

- report the spill to the teacher straight away
- wear eye protection/lab coat

- transfer the alkali using a pipette, burette or syringe – rather than pouring it from a beaker/measuring cylinder)

2 a Two from:

- spilling hot water
- clothing catching fire
- burning your hand on the Bunsen flame or beaker
- hot water splashing into your eyes or on your skin

You may have other suggestions, which you could discuss with your teacher; they may well be right!

b Two from:

- keeping the apparatus well away from edge of desk or other people
- not putting your hands near the flame or turning the Bunsen off and letting it cool before moving it; move the Bunsen by touching its base only; picking up a hot beaker using tongs or letting the beaker cool before moving it
- wearing eye protection and a lab coat.

You may have other suggestions, which you could discuss with your teacher; they may well be right!

3 a Flammable; **b** No smoking/no naked flames

4 Sam should stay at his desk and call for the teacher. If he left the spill, someone else might not notice it and come to harm because of it. If Sam stays at the desk, he can warn others.

5 Heating to high temperatures kills more of the bacteria. *If you spray things with disinfectant you can't be sure that all the surfaces have been covered, whereas the heat will get to all the parts of the equipment.*

6 She needs to lower the beaker into the stream without putting her hand in. She could tie a string around the lip of the beaker and make a handle. This means that her skin will not come into contact with the water, in case there is raw sewage in the stream or a poisonous chemical that is killing the fish. In addition/or you could suggest that she wears gloves, which will also prevent her skin coming into contact with the water.

S25 PRIMARY AND SECONDARY DATA

1 a Primary data is data that you have collected; secondary data is data that someone else has collected.

b Two from:

- you control the quality of the data
- you control what data is collected
- the data is up-to-date
- the data is relevant to your needs
- your conclusions are not affected by conclusions already drawn from the data.

2 a The factory owners used secondary data because they used data that someone else had collected.

b The data that shows the number of accidents in the first month of each quarter. *If you didn't know what 'a quarter' was you should have been able to work it out from the table. It's when a year is divided into four equal quarters starting with January, February and March.*

c The number of accidents per quarter.

d They probably drew the conclusion that the factory was getting safer (with fewer accidents) because that means that they don't have to spend extra money on safety. There is an alternative – that the factory owners wanted to shut the factory and were setting out to prove that it was getting too dangerous to operate. *As long as you have a good reason for your answer you will get the marks.*

e Use the number of accidents in the middle month of each quarter. *This figure stays at 20.*

S26 SYMBOLS AND CONVENTIONS

1 a $5 > 4$; **b** $2 + 2 = 4$; **c** $Mg + S \rightarrow MgS$

2 You should have drawn this with a ruler! Your drawing does not have to look exactly like the one below – it can have the different symbols in any order and in any position in the rectangle that shows the basic circuit.

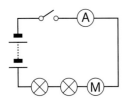

3 a nitrogen; **b** zinc; **c** radon; **d** tungsten; **e** gold

4 Five is greater than four; $5 > 4$:

- writing this as symbols took much less time
- the symbols are much clearer to understand/take less time to understand
- the symbols are understood all over the world.

5 The names need to be agreed by scientists all over the world, so that they all understand what a new symbol means.

6 a $2H_2 + O_2 \rightarrow 2H_2O$

If you haven't done symbol equations and balancing them yet you may have got this wrong. The little numbers show the atoms that are joined together. So H_2 means that there are two hydrogen atoms joined together. Hydrogen always exists like this and so you cannot change this. The big numbers show how many of a group of atoms you have. So $2H_2$ means that you have 2 lots of H_2 and this would contain a total of 4 atoms of hydrogen. $2H_2O$ means that you have 2 lots of H_2O. H_2O contains 2 hydrogens and 1 oxygen, so two lots of H_2O will give you 4 hydrogen atoms and 2 oxygen atoms. H_2O is the formula for water and you can't change the formula.

Start by writing out the symbols in your equation:

$H_2 + O_2 \rightarrow H_2O$

Then count the total number of one sort of atom on the left of the arrow and count them up on the right. Are they same? If not, you will need to add some big numbers into the equation to try to get the number of the atoms the same on each side of the arrow. Once you have done that you repeat the process for each of the atoms in your equation:

$2H_2 + O_2 \rightarrow 2H_2O$

If you got this first one wrong, go back and rewrite your answers for parts b, c and d before checking if you are correct.

b $CH_4 + 2O_2 \rightarrow CO_2 + 2H_2O$

c $6CO_2 + 6H_2O \rightarrow C_6H_{12}O_6 + 6O_2$

d $SnO_2 + 2H_2 \rightarrow Sn + 2H_2O$

S27 FRACTIONS, PERCENTAGES, RATIOS AND DECIMALS

1 a $\frac{1}{4}$ *the highest common factor is 3;*

 b $\frac{1}{2}$ *the highest common factor is 36*

 c $\frac{2}{9}$ *the highest common factor is 6*

 d $\frac{3}{10}$ *the highest common factor is 3*

2 100. *34% means '34 parts in 100' or $\frac{34}{100}$.*

3 The aluminium block is $\frac{14}{100}$ times the mass of the gold block.

4 There are 2 hydrogen atoms for each oxygen atom.

5 1:2. *Make sure that you haven't got this the wrong way round. The thing that you are comparing comes first, and the thing that you are comparing it to comes second. There is 1 carbon atom for each 2 oxygen atoms, so the ratio is 1:2.*

6 a 0.5 *You should recognise this one without having to work it out.*

 b 0.75 … *and this too;* **c** 0.68; **d** 0.4

7 a 50%; **b** 75%; **c** 68%; **d** 40%

8 1:1. *Remember that 2:2 is not as simple as it can be. You need to simplify ratios in the same way that you simplify fractions.*

9 $(5.99 - 5.06)/5.06 = 0.18379447 = 18.379447\%$

 A better answer is 18.4%, which has the same number of significant figures as the original data. See S18.

10 3:6 and 32:64 *Both can be simplified to 1/2.*

S28 MEAN, MEDIAN AND MODE

Don't forget the units!

1 a 3 cm; **b** 5 cm; **c** $\frac{30}{5} = 6$ cm

2 a 16.5 g; **b** 16.8 g; **c** $\frac{119}{7} = 17$ g

 *A better answer for **c** is 17.0 g – this states the answer to the same number of significant figures as in the original data. See S18.*

3 a The median. *In this case an average hotel is going to fall in the middle of all the other hotel ratings.*

 b The mean *You want to work out an estimate of the height of a Year 9 boy.*

 c The mode *You want to find out the favourite singers.*

S29 PROBABILITY

1 $\frac{1}{5}$, 0.5 or 50%. *If you are unsure about how to convert from fractions to decimals or percentages have a look at S27.*

2 a 0.25. *There is 1 chance in 4 of choosing a yellow tulip bulb; $1 \div 4 = 0.25$*

 b 0.75. *The probability of planting a blue tulip is 0.25 (the same as for a yellow tulip in **a**; and so the probability of not planting it is $1 - 0.25 = 0.75$.*

3 a 0.04 (or $\frac{1}{25}$ or 4%). *There is 1 chance in 25 of choosing a certain letter; $1 \div 25 = 0.04$.*

 b 0.96 (or $\frac{24}{25}$ or 96%). *The probability of choosing a T is 0.04 (the same as for choosing an X in **a**); so the probability of not choosing it is $1 - 0.04 = 0.96$.*

 c 0.2 (or $\frac{5}{25}$ or 20%). *There are five letters from A to E and a total of 25 possibilities; $5 \div 25 = 0.2$*

 d 1 (or 100%)

S30 TABLES

1

Flavour of crisps	Students in 11 F with that favourite
salt & vinegar	11
ready salted	7
cheese & onion	6
smoky bacon	3
prawn cocktail	2
other	1

It is now much easier to see how popular the different flavours of crisps are. The table was originally in alphabetical order.

2 a

Height groups above sea level (m)	Number of rabbits found at that height
200–249	2
250–299	3
300–349	2
350–399	2
400–449	1
450–500	2

To start with you need to decide on your height groups, which must all be the same size. Start by finding the lowest reading and the highest, and then divide this range into equal chunks.

You need to make sure that your groups do not overlap. Then you need to write your groups in order in your table. Make sure that you have not forgotten the units in the heading.

Finally add up the numbers of rabbits in each height group and complete the table. You might find this easier to do as a 'tally', crossing each reading out as you put it into a rough 'tally' chart:

Height groups above sea level (m)	Tally
200–249	/ /
250–299	/ / /
300–349	/ /
350–399	/ /
400–449	/
450– 500	/ /

  b Trends and patterns are easier to see if data is put in order.

3 a The range is 5 minutes, the interval is 1 minute, the independent variable is the time and the dependent variable is the temperature.

  b The longer the water is heated, the higher the temperature it has.

S31 BAR CHARTS

1 a 30°C; **b** 33°C or 34°C

2 Your bar chart should have:

- a title – e.g. amount of vitamin C in different fruits
- the dependent variable on the *y*-axis – amount of vitamin C
- the independent variable on the *x*-axis – the type of fruit
- a good scale for the *y*-axis so that the plotted points are well spread
- a *y*-axis scale that has even divisions
- a *y*-axis scale that is numbered
- a label for the *x*-axis – e.g. fruit
- a label for each bar on the *x*-axis – e.g. mango, kiwi fruit, …

- gaps between the *x*-axis bars
- an *x*-axis scale that has even divisions
- all bars plotted accurately
- all bars the same width
- all bars neatly drawn with a ruler.

The names of fruits on the *x*-axis ordered alphabetically or the fruits ordered by amount of vitamin C.

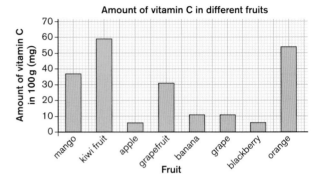

3 a The type of crisp. *It is the type of crisp's frequency of being favourite that you are measuring.*

  b Salt & vinegar and cheese & onion

  c You can see at a glance where the tallest bars are – you don't have to look at every piece of data to compare it with the others.

S32 FREQUENCY DIAGRAMS

1 a

Height groups (cm)	Number of 4 year-olds in that height group
90–94.9	1
95–99.9	3
100–104.9	7
105–109.9	8
110–114.9	1

  b Number of 4 year olds/frequency.

2 One from:

- the most common eruption time is between 100 and 105 seconds
- it is unusual for the length of an eruption to be longer than 115 seconds
- most eruptions last between 100 and 115 seconds.

There are lots of different things that this histogram tells you. When you use a histogram it is usually to present evidence to support a point that you are making – and so exactly what you say about a histogram depends on the point you want to make.

3 *Note that you are drawing a bar chart frequency diagram here (and not a histogram) because the groups you are using are of discrete data – that is data that can only have a certain range of values – and not a continuous range. People come in whole numbers – you can't have 0.3 of a person on a bus!*

Your frequency diagram should have:

- a title
- the dependent variable on the *y*-axis – number of times
- the independent variable on the *x*-axis – your groups
- a good scale for the *y*-axis so that the plotted points are well spread
- a *y*-axis scale that has even divisions
- a *y*-axis scale that is numbered
- a label for the *x*-axis – number of people on the 391 bus
- a label for each group on the *x*-axis – e.g. 1–5
- gaps between the *x*-axis bar groups
- all bars plotted accurately
- all bars the same width
- all bars neatly drawn with a ruler.

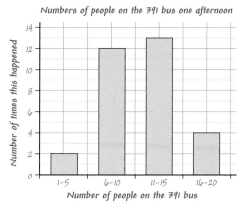

Numbers of people on the 391 bus one afternoon

4 *The first problem you face in drawing a histogram is to divide the independent variable up into groups. You need to make sure that your groups do not overlap; if they do then there may be readings that could go into more than one group. The choice of group size is up to you but for this question, it's a good idea to use the council's group size for trees to cut in 5 years time (i.e. a group size of 2 m).*

Your histogram should have:

- a title

- the dependent variable on the *y*-axis – number of trees
- the independent variable on the *x*-axis – your groups
- a good scale for the *y*-axis so that the plotted points are well spread
- a *y*-axis scale that has even divisions
- a *y*-axis scale that is numbered
- a label for the *x*-axis – e.g. height
- no gaps between the *x*-axis bar groups
- an *x*-axis scale that has even divisions
- all bars plotted accurately
- all bars the same width
- all bars neatly drawn with a ruler.

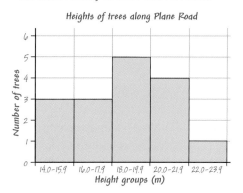

Heights of trees along Plane Road

5 For the people with different jobs earning different amounts of money, you would use a bar chart because the independent variable (the one that you are selecting values for) is discrete data. For the other data set you would use a histogram because the independent variable (the amount of money) is continuous. *You would then need to divide the amounts of money into groups in order to draw the histogram.*

S33 LINE GRAPHS

Don't forget the units!

1 a Independent variable = time; dependent variable = temperature

  b 2°C; **c** 0.4°C; **d** 16.4°C; **e** 9.6°C; **f** 13.6°C... *but anywhere between 13.4 and 13.8°C is OK ... provided you haven't forgotten the units!*

2 *The difficulty with this question is that you need to make sure that you develop an even scale for the x-axis because the intervals at which the measurements are made are not equal. Time, on the x-axis, needs to run at a steady rate and so the scale must remain the same.*

Your line graph should have:
- a title
- the dependent variable on the *y*-axis – mean systolic blood pressure
- the independent variable on the *x*-axis – time
- a good scale for the *y*-axis so that the plotted points are well spread
- a *y*-axis scale that has even divisions
- a *y*-axis scale that is numbered
- a label for the *y*-axis with units –systolic blood pressure (mmHg)

You might have written 'blood pressure' or 'systolic blood pressure' but to be absolutely correct you should write 'mean systolic blood pressure'. If you don't know what this means have a look at S28.

- a good scale for the *x*-axis so that the plotted points are well spread
- a label for the *x*-axis with units – time after exercise (min)
- an *x*-axis scale that has even divisions
- an *x*-axis scale that is numbered
- all points plotted accurately
- all points plotted neatly
- points connected with straight lines, drawn with a ruler.

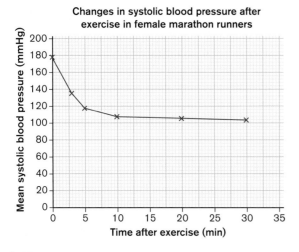

Changes in systolic blood pressure after exercise in female marathon runners

b There are two main reasons:
- the variables are both continuous – so you wouldn't use a bar chart
- the dependent variable is not a frequency – so you wouldn't use a histogram.

You'll also get some credit if you explain that you cannot see how something changes gradually over time if you were to use a bar chart or a histogram. A line graph will let you see the gradual trend.

S34 SCATTER GRAPHS

1 a The independent variable is height; the dependent variable is age. *Remember to say which is which … don't just write down 'height and age'.*

b 10 cm intervals; **c** The older he gets, the taller he becomes; **d** 160 cm

2 a Your scatter graph should have:

- a title
- the dependent variable on the *y*-axis – time for one orbit. *Remember that in a table, the first column shows the independent variable and the others show measurements of the dependent variable. See S30.)*
- the independent variable on the *x*-axis – distance from Sun
- a good scale for the *y*-axis so that the plotted points are well spread
- a *y*-axis scale that has even divisions
- a *y*-axis scale that is numbered
- a label for the *y*-axis with units
- a good scale for the *x*-axis so that the plotted points are well spread
- a label for the *x*-axis with units
- an *x*-axis scale that has even divisions
- an *x*-axis scale that is numbered
- all points plotted accurately
- all points plotted neatly.

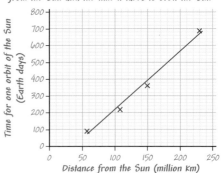

Correlation between the distance of the inner planets from the Sun and the time it takes to orbit the Sun

b The further a planet is from the Sun, the longer it takes to go around the Sun.

c *Shown on the graph above.*

3 A line graph is normally used to show how something changes with time. Here we are looking for a correlation between two variables and so a scatter graph is used.

S35 GRADIENTS

1 a 140 cm at 9 years old; 160 cm at 12 years old. *Remember that these are estimates because his height wasn't measured at exactly 9 or 12 years old. We are using the line through the points to estimate those values.*

b Gradient = $\dfrac{\text{change in } y}{\text{change in } x}$

$= \dfrac{(160 - 140)}{(12 - 9)}$

$= \dfrac{20}{3}$

$= 6.7$

Even if you got the answer wrong you may get some marks for showing your working ... so don't forget to show it!

c cm/year

d No because the line does not go through the origin. *This makes sense if you think about it because when you are born you are already a certain height.*

2 a Yes because the line goes through the origin.

b The equation for a straight line that goes through the origin will be $y = mx$. The gradient, m, is 20. So $y = 20x$. *Note that the question asks you to give the equation in terms of x and y, which means that you can't have m (or c) in it. You can check that your answer is right by picking a value of x and then looking back at the graph. So, when x = 1.5 seconds, y = 20x = (20 × 1.5) = 30. Checking back on the graph, when x = 1.5 seconds, y = 30.*

3 a No because the line does not go through the origin.

b $y = mx + c$, where c is where the line crosses the y-axis, which is at 32; and m is the gradient:

gradient = $\dfrac{\text{change in } y}{\text{change in } x}$

$= \dfrac{(86 - 50)}{(30 - 10)}$

$= \dfrac{36}{20}$

$= 1.8$

So $y = 1.8x + 32$

There are several things to note here. First, you don't need to use the exact points that we've chosen here to calculate the gradient. You can use any two points you like – but they should be points that you can clearly and easily read from the graph. Second, you should always show all your working. It may get you some marks even if you get the answer wrong. And last, note that the equation for the line is the equation for converting any temperature in degrees Celsius into degrees Fahrenheit – i.e. °F = (1.8 ×°C) + 32.

S36 PIE CHARTS

1 The salt & vinegar flavour has the biggest share of the pie.

2 Make sure you have:

- a title
- used compasses or similar to draw the circle
- labelled all the categories neatly
- the correct angles
- used a ruler to draw the lines..

Electricity use in a UK house

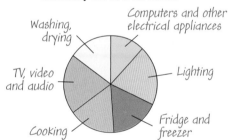

3 *You've been asked to draw a pie chart for this data because you are showing the different proportions that things contribute to a whole.*

The angles you need are calculated like this:

Gas	Nitrogen	Oxygen	Other	Total
Percentage	78.1	21.0	0.9	100
angle calculation $= \dfrac{360}{\text{total}}$ $= \dfrac{360}{100}$ $= 3.6$	78.1 × 3.6	21.0 × 3.6	0.9 × 3.6	
angle	281°	76°	3°	360°

Make sure you have:

- a title
- used compasses or similar to draw the circle
- labelled all the categories neatly
- the correct angles
- used a ruler to draw the lines.

Proportions of the different gases in air

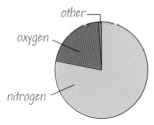

4 *You've been asked to draw a pie chart for this data because you are showing the different proportions that things contribute to a whole.*

The angles you need are calculated like this:

Amount of time online	7+ hours	3–7 hours	1–3 hours	<1 hour	Total
Number of people	3	17	33	37	90
angle calculation $= \frac{360}{\text{total}}$ $= \frac{360}{90}$ $= 4$	3 × 4	17 × 4	33 × 4	37 × 4	
Angle	12°	68°	132°	148°	360°

Make sure you have:

- a title
- used a compass or similar to draw the circle
- labelled all the categories neatly
- the correct angles
- used a ruler to draw the lines.

Internet use per day

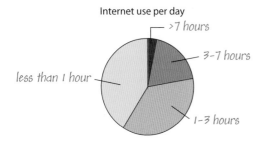

5 It's very difficult to see how the share of energy use has changed on the pie charts. *If you plotted this on a grouped bar chart you could compare each sector in each year as bars side by side, making it easier to see if their share had changed. Have a look at the bar chart below to help you understand this.*

How energy use in Scotland has changed

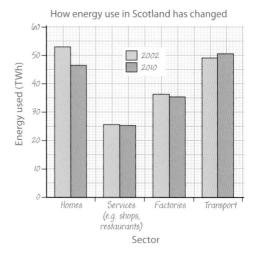

The grouped bar chart shows that the share of total energy used by homes has dropped quite a bit between these two years and the share of total energy used by transport has increased. It's difficult to see this on the two pie charts.

S37 VENN DIAGRAMS

1 Figure A: there are no animals that are also plants.

Figure B: some languages have a word that means both 'hello' and 'goodbye'.

Figure C: all alkalis are found in a larger group of chemicals called bases.

2 There is no music that both Kaito and Drew like.

3

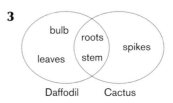

Daffodil   Cactus

4

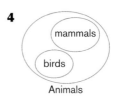

Animals

5

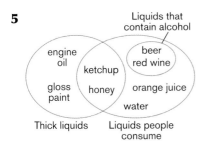

6

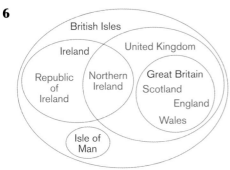

S38 PRESENTING DATA

1 A: scatter graph; B: table; C: line graph; D: histogram; E: Venn diagram; F: bar chart; G: pie chart; H: flow chart; I: frequency diagram

2 *You'll need to draw a histogram because we are interested in the number of rabbits at certain heights (frequency,) and the heights to be grouped are continuous data.*

The first problem you face in drawing a histogram is to divide the independent variable into groups. You need to make sure that your groups do not overlap; if they do then there may be readings that could go into more than one group.

Your histogram should have:

- a title
- the dependent variable on the *y*-axis – numbers
- the independent variable on the *x*-axis – your groups
- a good scale for the *y*-axis so that the plotted points are well spread
- a *y*-axis scale that has even divisions
- a *y*-axis scale that is numbered
- a label for the *x*-axis – e.g. heights
- no gaps between the *x*-axis bar groups
- an *x*-axis scale that has even divisions
- all bars are plotted accurately
- all bars are the same width
- all bars are drawn neatly with a ruler.

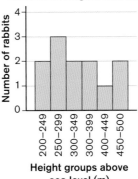

Numbers of rabbits found at different heights on a hill

3 a The crisp flavour data could be presented as an ordered table, two pie charts or a grouped bar chart (or two bar charts). The grouped bar chart would be best to identify the favourite flavours of crisps in the two classes at a glance because the tallest column for each class will be obvious. *For the pie charts it will be difficult to tell the difference between cheese & onion and salt & vinegar for class 11B because they have very similar numbers of students. For the table, you could order it by favourite crisps in one class, but that would mean that the favourite flavour in the other class is not at the top of the table.*

b Histogram for the heights because the independent variable is continuous data that has been divided into groups and the dependent variable is a frequency. Line graph for the data in Figure B because you are following the changes of a variable with time.

S39 DRAWING CONCLUSIONS

1 QWC *You just need to reorder the sentences.*

The car goes fastest on the smoothest surface. *This is what Kenny found out.*

This was because there is less friction on smoother surfaces. *This is Kenny's explanation for why this happens.*

The car went 2 m/s on the wooden surface, which is faster than on the other surfaces. The wood was the smoothest surface. *This is Kenny's evidence.*

My prediction was that if the car is on a smoother slope then it will go faster. My prediction was right. *This is how Kenny's prediction compared with his findings.*

2 a Her results do not agree with her prediction. *The temperature increases are different for each wood.*

b No. There is no evidence in her results about the masses of the wood, only the volumes. She is drawing a conclusion that cannot be drawn from the results.

An even better answer would also point out that she has not used very scientific words – using 'mass' is a much better way of talking about how 'heavy' something is. And 'temperature rise' is better than talking about 'heating up'. *There are reasons behind this. When people talk about 'heaviness' they are often talking about 'weight'. 'Mass' and 'weight' are not the same. And 'temperature' and 'heat' (which is a form of energy) are not the same either. It doesn't matter whether or not you understand those reasons, just remember to use scientific terms in your writing.*

3 The number of crimes had increased or more crime was being reported.

4 *There are many possible hypotheses here. How many did you get?*
- The poison was killing the birds.
- The poison was killing the things that the birds ate for food.
- The poison was killing the things that another predator ate for food, which meant that the predator had to eat the birds instead.
- There was a rise in predators.

S40 MODELS

1 a Hold a piece of string between two points so that it was stretched and taut.

b Put one ball on the ground and then put other balls at different distances from it.

c Place some balls on the ground with lots of space between them.

d You can see the models and see what happens in them. *You cannot usually see light beams travelling, you can't see the whole of the Solar System and you can't see particles.*

2 21 m/7 s = 3 m/s *Don't forget the units!*

3 a sodium + chlorine → sodium chloride

b This model does not show us *how* the reaction happens.

4 Yes. You can see the gaps between the particles and so understand that the particles could be squashed into smaller space.

5 a

Part in electric circuit	Represented in central heating system by …	Represented in food conveyer system by …
cell (battery)	boiler and pump	chef
wires	pipes	conveyer
lamp	radiator	diner

b *There are many strengths and weaknesses that you can write about and how many you get will depend on how much study you have done of electric circuits. You are not expected to get all the points listed below but if you get one strength and one weakness for each you are doing well. And you may have got some strengths/weaknesses that are not listed below.*

Strengths of the central heating system model include:
- energy is given out by the radiator just like it is by the lamp (although the two forms of energy are different)
- the energy is carried by flowing water, just like the energy is carried by flowing particles (electrons) in a wire
- the boiler and pump components give energy to the water, just like the cell gives energy to the particles (electrons) flowing in the wire
- the boiler and pump provides the 'push' to move the water along, just like the cell provides the push to move the particles (electrons)
- the pipes are always full of water, just like wires are always full of particles (electrons)
- no water is lost as it flows around the circuit, just like no particles (electrons) are lost from the wires.

Weaknesses of the central heating system model include:
- when you switch on a circuit, energy is instantly released from the lamp, but a radiator takes time to get hot.
- a cell makes a current flow and provides the energy carried by the particles, but a central heating system needs two parts to do this – a boiler and a pump

- the energy supplied by the cell is all released by the lamp, but the radiator only releases some of the energy in the water into a room
- the lamp transfers electrical energy to heat and light energy, but in the radiator the form of the energy remains the same – heat

Strengths of the food conveyer system model include:

- energy (as food) is taken from the conveyer by the diner, just like a lamp takes energy from the wires
- the diner transfers the chemical energy in food into many other types of energy in the body, just like the lamp transfers electrical energy to heat and light energy
- the energy is carried by a moving conveyer, just like the energy is carried by flowing particles (electrons) in a wire
- the chef puts packets of food (energy) on the conveyer, just like the cell gives energy to the particles (electrons) flowing in the wire

Weaknesses of the food conveyer system model include:

- the chef puts the food (energy) on the conveyer, but the chef does not make the conveyer go round – that's done by a separate motor
- the lamp transfers energy immediately, but the diner transfers energy from food very slowly in comparison
- the energy supplied by the cell is all released by the lamp, but the diner only eats some of the food from the conveyer

6 a If you throw a table tennis ball at a flat surface at a certain angle, it will bounce off the surface at the same angle … just like light. Using string, you would have to measure the angles.

   b Light moves in straight lines, but table tennis balls fall to the ground as they get slower. *You might have said that light is not divided up into balls. That's fine for now but you will find out later on in your studies of physics that light can behave as both a wave and as little packets of energy. Most strange!*

7 *There are many strengths and weaknesses that you can write about it and how many you get will depend on how much study you have done of the heart. You are not expected to get all the points listed below but if you get two strengths and two weaknesses you are*

doing very well. And you may have got some strengths/weaknesses that are not listed below.

Strengths:

- As you pull a bicycle pump, its inner chamber expands and so fills with air – just like the chambers of the heart when the muscles relax.
- As you push a bicycle pump, its inner chamber is made smaller and so air is squashed out – just like the chambers of the heart when the muscle contracts.
- A bicycle pump contains a valve to stop air flowing in the wrong direction – just like the heart contains valves.

Weaknesses:

- A bicycle pump has only one chamber – a heart has four.
- A bicycle pump needs an external force to operate it – the heart generates its own force in its muscles.
- A bicycle pump is pumping air, which can be squashed – unlike blood, which cannot.
- Only one part of the pump changes the volume inside the pump's chamber – in the heart, all of a chamber's walls move.

8 $S = \frac{D}{T}$ and so $D = S \times T$. There are 60 minutes in one hour, so 15 minutes $= \frac{15}{60} = 0.25$ hours. $D = S \times T$, and so $D = 204 \times 0.25 = 51\,km$.

This question illustrates the importance of showing your working and of using units. You'll get some credit even if you forgot to convert minutes into hours.

S41 ARGUMENTS

1 a **QWC** B, C and D

   b **QWC** Sentence D asks a question of the reader and sentence E uses emotive language. *Asking a question in this style is called a' rhetorical' question. It's a question that doesn't expect an answer and is used for impact. In sentence E, you could just as well have written 'Animals perform tricks' but using powerful adjectives is much more persuasive.*

   c **QWC** *Judge your argument against the following points. The points further down the list are the ones that are more difficult to include.*

★ You state that you are in favour of or against using animals in circuses.

★ You give a reason for being in favour of animals in circuses – e.g. the animals always have enough healthy food.

★★ You explain one or more reasons in favour of using animals – e.g. the animals always have enough healthy food because scientists have learnt what the animals need in their diet.

★★ You explain one or more reasons against using animals e.g. tigers are used to walking for a long time each day but if they are in a cage they cannot do this.

★★ Each different reason for your opinion has its own paragraph.

★★★ Each different reason for your opinion is supported by evidence.

★★★ You have used persuasive language – e.g. putting a question to the reader, using emotive words, repeating evidence, exaggeration.

★★★ You write a counterargument.

★★★ You write a clear response to one counterargument – e.g. some people might say the animals can always get enough healthy food, but that is only if the circus has enough money to buy food or if the trainers do not withhold food from the animals as a punishment.

2 **QWC** *There are many ways in which you could argue in favour of uniforms. Here is one example – it has been broken down into the various parts to show how a writing frame has been used.*

"I think that school uniforms are an excellent idea and all schools should have a uniform." *This is the statement of what the person thinks (the opinion).*

"Having a uniform means that poor students are not obvious because a uniform makes everyone look the same." *This is the first reason for the person's opinion. The underlined part shows the evidence used to support the reason.*

"Also, clothes can be really expensive, especially the ones from brands. For example, my Hugo Boss trousers that my Mum bought me for smart cost £70. This is over twice what a whole uniform could cost for me. So it makes it easier for most people to afford if everyone has a set uniform." *The second reason has its own paragraph. Again it has evidence to support the reason.*

"If everyone in the country has a similar uniform then so many pairs of trousers will be needed that they will be even cheaper to make and this will bring the price down even more." *The third reason has its own paragraph.*

"Some people might say that uniforms are still too expensive but you can easily buy second hand uniforms in charity shops." *This paragraph contains the counter argument. The underlined text is the response to the counterargument.*

"So, it is sensible to have uniform because it makes everyone the same and doesn't cost too much." *Finally, the person finishes with a short summary, stating the opinion again.*

Of course there are other reasons for and against school uniforms that your argument could use instead of the ones above. For example:

- A uniform means that everyone in the school looks smart and creates a good impression.
- A uniform means that students can't compete with each other as to who has the most expensive things.
- Uniforms don't last very long because the material is not of good quality.

3 **QWC** Not everyone thinks that the fine system is a good idea. Former Health Secretary Edwina Currie said: "Personally I'd prefer that huge sum to be spent on extra staff, not on a fine."

Response: However, in Leeds the money is not taken out of funding for a hospital; the amount of the fine is the amount that now has to be spent on tackling the issue.

S42 EVALUATING

1 a The results show an increase in temperature when the nails reacted with the acid and so he has concluded that the reaction causes a temperature rise.

b **QWC** *You could check the results against each of the bullet points on page 49 in S42.*

- The investigation is not valid because the results do not allow you to answer the question. The nails are rusty so it could be that the rust is reacting with the acid to cause the temperature increase and not the iron.
- The results are valid because they measure a temperature increase. *This is what was supposed to be measured.*
- One of the results is very different from the other two and might be anomalous.
- The results are not very repeatable since two results are close but one is very different. *There are no results from other groups so it's*

impossible to say if the results are reproducible.

- So far as we can tell, the results have been collected in an unbiased way (a fair test should have been done).
- You could improve these results by doing more repeat readings.

c [QWC] *You could check the results against each of the bullet points on page 49 in S42.*

- All the readings showed a temperature increase so there are probably enough readings to draw that conclusion. *You couldn't say how much the temperature increase should be because there are only three readings, one of which is very different from the other two. However, you can say that all the readings showed an increase for the reaction that was tested.*
- However, the conclusion is not valid because it does not draw from the results. The results may be for the reaction between rust and acid and not between iron and acid.
- The conclusion is biased. *It's trying to get you to think that the reaction between iron and acid causes a temperature rise but that is probably not the reaction that has occurred.*

S43 CHANGING SCIENTIFIC IDEAS

1 a [QWC] Introduction. *This is the part of an investigation report where you write about why you are doing your investigation and what knowledge you have used to think up your ideas that you are going to test.*

b Conclusion. *That's what we can say from the results.*

c References.

d Method. *This is part of an equipment list.*

e Results.

2 So that they can be understood easily by scientists all over the world.

3 a You can find out quickly if a paper contains the information that you are interested in. OR it allows you to search easily for papers that might interest you.

b [QWC] *An abstract is an overview, which means that it needs to be a very brief summary of the report. It should include a brief statement of the hypothesis and a brief statement about what*

was discovered:

We tested the hypothesis that the amount of current depends on the length of the wire. By using resistance wire, we showed that the longer the wire, the less current there was

4 The results show all the data that has been collected; the conclusion explains what you can tell from the results.

5 a Three

b The last one – *Velociraptors* were afraid of *Tenontosaurus* dinosaurs.

6 a One or both of:

- Professor Fry because he is a professor.
- Professor Fry because he has written a paper in a journal, and so his paper has been peer-reviewed.

b To give what she says more 'weight'. *If people put 'doctor' in front of their names when they are writing about medical issues then people often assume that they are medical doctors (and not PhD doctors). People assume that a medical doctor knows more about foods than someone who is not a medical doctor.*

c *You should have outlined the peer review process showing in Figure B on page 50 in S43.* The paper is sent to the editor of a journal. The editor checks the paper and sends it to scientists working on similar things, who have expert knowledge. The scientists review the paper and then tell the editor whether it should or should not be published (and whether or not anything in it needs changing). The editor then decides whether to publish or not.

S44 BENEFITS, DRAWBACKS AND IMPLICATIONS

1 One benefit from: no carbon dioxide produced; the wind won't run out (is renewable).

One drawback from: may harm wildlife (e.g. flying birds); may cause noise pollution; may ruin the look of the countryside; may be a hazard to shipping (if built out at sea); doesn't produce electricity if there is no wind.

One implication from: if we build more wind farms we will need to import less fossil fuel; we will create jobs in the manufacture and installation of the turbines.

There are other benefits, drawbacks and implications that you might have instead of those listed here. And you might have an implication that is either a benefit or a drawback. That's fine – you just need to make sure that your implication is a knock-on effect as opposed to a direct effect. For example, a direct effect of wind turbines is the noise that they make. An implication of this is that the value of people's homes in the area may fall or that numbers of a certain animal may fall because the noise worries them.

2 a *Note that in this question you are asked to explain the benefits, drawbacks and implications – not just state what they are. So you need to give a reason why a benefit is a benefit, etc.*

Endoscope

- Benefit – allows doctors to see inside the body so that they can find out what is wrong; allows doctors to position surgical implements during an operation without having to cut the patient open completely so that the patient recovers faster from the operation; gives a very clear image of the inside of the body that contains more detail than an ultrasound or CT scan; does not need the doctors to be screened from the machine because harmful radiation is not being used).
- Drawback – the doctors can only see a small bit of the inside of the body at any one time and so it takes longer to look at a larger area than using a scanner; involves pushing something into the body which might damage that part of the body or might carry an infection into the body; difficult to operate precisely.
- Implication – more operations can be done because people recover from operations more quickly; the hospital has to spend money on endoscope equipment. *See the comments in the answer to question* **1** *about what makes a good implication.*

Ultrasound scanner

- Benefit – allows doctors to see inside the body without going into the body.
- Drawback – the image is not always very clear and so smaller problems may be missed.
- Implication – many people can have quick scans immediately using ultrasound

equipment so it cuts waiting times for scans that take longer, such as CT scans.

CT scanner

- Benefit – provides detailed images of a large portion of the body so that a large area can be scanned for problems.
- Drawback – uses X-rays and people who operate the machinery need to be shielded from it.
- Implication – it is expensive equipment and so the hospital has less money to spend on other things.

b Possible criteria include: How much does it cost? How many people will it help? What training do staff need to operate it? How quick is it? *'Criteria' are statements that you use to judge things. So, in this case, imagine you were in charge of a large hospital and think about how you would decide whether or not to buy any of these pieces of equipment, remembering that the hospital has only a limited amount of money.*

S45 RISKS AND DECISIONS

1 a & b *Remember that a hazard is anything that can cause harm – but you'll need to say what that harm is. A risk is the likelihood of harm happening from that hazard. There are ten hazards and ways of reducing their risks as shown in the table below. You might even have spotted some more hazards!*

Hazard	Way of reducing the risk
One running student can bump into another and spill something	Don't run in the lab
If you eat in the lab you might eat poisonous chemicals	Don't eat in the lab
If you lean over heating apparatus you might get burnt	Heat things at a distance from you
Bags lying on the ground can be tripped over	Put all bags away
If you heat a test tube strongly hot chemicals can shoot out of the open end and burn	Point the open ends of heated test tubes away from people

Hazard	Way of reducing the risk
Long hair can catch fire on Bunsen burners	Tie back long hair.
Poking things into an electrical socket can give you an electric shock	Do not put anything into an electrical socket
Liquids on the flood can be slipped on.	Mop up any spills straight away
Broken glass can cut people	Tell a teacher if something gets broken so that it can be cleared away safety and quickly
Some chemicals are harmful and should not sniffed	Look carefully at the hazard labels on chemical bottles and follow any safety instructions on the bottles

2 a The screen would be better because this will prevent everyone touching the inner hot parts of the boiler. Small children and people who do not speak English may not read a sign or know what it means.

b The symbol can be understood by people all over the world, even if they do not speak English.

3 A hazard of a hot cup or glass is that it can damage your skin. The risk of this happening is reduced by having a cup with a handle.

S46 DECISIONS ABOUT SCIENCE

1 • Financial costs – how much will it cost the company?
• Cost to the environment –how will we dispose of the phones when they are old?
• Effect on people – does the phone have the right functions for everyone in the company?
• Ethics and morals – can we be sure the phones are not made using child labour?

2 a One from:

• some people think it is wrong to look at dead bodies
• the unborn child in the photo did not have a choice whether or not to be on display
• the display might give people nightmares

• religious views prevent looking at dead bodies
• religious views oppose the cutting up of dead bodies.

b Because it was thought to benefit more people than it would cause problems for. *An ethical decision is usually based on the best outcome for the greatest number of people. In this case, organisers decided that a lot of people would learn more about the human body by seeing the exhibition and those who opposed the exhibition would not need to go and see it.*

3 Two from:

• people want computers/phones that can go faster – so companies that make faster chips can earn more money
• if a chip uses less power, the battery will last longer and people want this – so companies that make more efficient chips can earn more money
• if a chip uses less power it will need less resources to produce the power to power it – there is an environmental benefit.

S47 SCIENCE IN THE MEDIA

1 a QWC That they are unsafe.

b QWC That the government is failing/doesn't care/isn't very good on health matters.

c QWC The problems with MRSA, a very dangerous bacterium, are increasing in British hospitals. *You might have phrased your answer differently but that's essentially what it says.*

d QWC Two of:

• by using emotive language – for example, words like 'death trap', 'superbug', 'killer', 'grim', 'shocking' are all designed to make you feel shock
• by using repetition – for example, the idea of patients being put at risk is repeated three times
• by using questions that have no real answer but which are designed to get you to agree with the article – for example, 'How can we take this government seriously on health?

e QWC You should have evaluated the article against these points:

• Meaning: it is clear in its meaning.
• Up-to-date: the information was when this book was published!

- Grammar and spelling: in the last line it should say '...this government's broken...'. There is an apostrophe missing.
- Good quality data: data from the Health Protection Agency is good.
- Evidence for claims: there is evidence for the claims but this is highly biased. Of the 162 NHS trusts in the UK, data is only presented for one trust. *Actually, the total numbers of MRSA cases across all trusts fell steadily from 2007 to 2011. This is like doing an experiment and picking one anomalous result to base your conclusions on. This decrease in MRSA cases is the reverse of what the article wants you to believe.*
- Reveal sources of information: the article does this.
- Sides of a debate: the article does not present both sides of the debate.

Note that the first letter of each of these points (criteria) spells out MUGGERS. You could try to remember this for evaluating other articles.

2 **QWC** There are various examples of persuasive language in the advert:

- repetition: the advert repeats the word 'white' and the idea that White-Daze whites are better over and over again
- emotive language: words used such as 'bright', 'brilliant', 'sparkling'
- using the pronoun 'we': at the start of the last paragraph
- asking questions that have no real answer: So why settle for anything less than white?
- using phrases: 'It goes without saying' at the start of the first paragraph.

3 a **QWC** That there was no evidence to support the BCA's opinion.

b The BCA felt that Simon Singh had damaged its reputation. *When people write things about others that are untrue and may damage their reputations, it is called 'libel'.*

c The BCA did not provide evidence to support their opinion so they could not show that Simon Singh was wrong.

1 a 162

b 8 *This is worked out by $2 \times \frac{400}{100} = 2 \times 4 = 8$. Remember that a percentage is a fraction in which the denominator is 100. If you had difficulty with this, have a look at S27.*

c MRSA is a big problem in UK hospitals and the government is not very good at health.

d MRSA is becoming less of a problem in UK hospitals and a system of fines will help to improve things still further.

e Some hospitals still have a problem with MRSA.

f The writer of the first article (on page 57) has only used a very small part of the data – the data from one NHS trust. The writer of the second article (on page 58) has used the figures for all NHS trusts.

g From the second one (on page 58). This is because the article describes how there has been a continuous decrease in the number of infections. The first article only gives two figures – one for the start of 2008 and the other for the start of 2011. *The first writer has done this to make you think that there has been a continual rise in MRSA infections in this hospital. In fact, this isn't the case. The real numbers of infections in Dartford & Gravesham are shown in the table below.*

Year	Time period	MRSA infections in Dartford & Gravesham NHS trust	MRSA infections in all NHS trusts
2008	Jan–Mar	2	970
	Apr–Jun	3	839
	Jul–Sep	6	724
	Oct–Dec	8	678
2009	Jan–Mar	5	694
	Apr–Jun	2	510
	Jul–Sep	2	462

Year	Time period	MRSA infections in Dartford & Gravesham NHS trust	MRSA infections in all NHS trusts
	Oct–Dec	4	443
2010	Jan–Mar	2	483
	Apr –Jun	3	421
	Jul–Sep	1	395
	Oct–Dec	1	331
2011	Jan–Mar	8	334

By choosing just two figures out of an set of data, it's possible to imply things that are not really in the data.

S49 NOTE-TAKING AND FORMAL WRITING

1 a QWC Point: hospitals are winning the fight against MRSA infections.

Evidence: new figures of number of infections.

Explanation: these show that in the first quarter of 2008 there were 970 MRSA infection cases, but this dropped fairly steadily until in the first quarter of 2011 the number was 334.

b QWC Main idea: progress is being made against MRSA.

- MRSA infections coming down. New figures of MRSA infections show a steady drop.
- There are still some problems – e.g. Leeds Teaching Hospitals had 21 cases in the first part of 2011.
- Fines to help solve remaining problems – e.g. Leeds Teaching Hospitals to be fined £400 000.
- Not everyone likes fines but fines will not take money from funding.
- Conclusion: Great progress, but room for improvement.

You might have put your notes in a different format and that does not matter. The thing to remember is that they are your notes and they need to make up a summary of the article, which then allows you to remember what the article said.

c QWC Ideas include: making the sentences much shorter; taking out the long words; explaining words like 'bacteria' or leaving them out; making the article much shorter.

d QWC MRSA is a germ that can cause people problems in hospitals. So, hospitals have worked hard to stop people getting this. The hard work has had an effect and the number of people getting MRSA in hospitals has been going down in the last few years. Hospitals that still have too much MRSA may get fined and this should help the people in those hospitals work even harder to get rid of MRSA.

There is no right or wrong answer to this question but you should have tried to have used some of the techniques from part c to rewrite the article.

2 QWC Some points that you could have made:

- There are conventions that people expect – which make it easier to compare one piece of writing with another.
- Your audience needs to understand what you are telling them – otherwise it's pointless telling them!
- You want people to enjoy what you have to say – different people enjoy different things.

EARTHQUAKE PREDICTING

1 They suddenly decreased.

2 Your line graph should have:

- a title
- the dependent variable on the *y*-axis – number of male toads
- the independent variable on the *x*-axis – date (2009)
- a good scale for the *y*-axis so that the plotted points are well spread
- a *y*-axis scale that has even divisions
- a *y*-axis scale that is numbered
- a good scale for the *x*-axis so that the plotted points are well spread
- a label for the *x*-axis
- an *x*-axis scale that has even divisions
- an *x*-axis scale that is numbered
- all points plotted accurately
- all points plotted neatly
- points each connected with straight lines, drawn with a ruler.

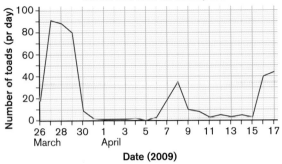

The number of toads by a lake before and after an earthquake.

Date (2009)

3 6th April 2009. *That's the highest bar on the bar chart and the caption tells you that the lower bars are due to shocks before and after the main earthquake.*

4 What did the toads detect that made them leave the lake?

5 a A hypothesis

b If you make a lake/pond more acidic then toads will leave the water. Or, if there is an earthquake in an area then ponds and lakes will get more acidic beforehand.

6 $91 - 0 = 91$. *The range is the difference between the highest and the lowest readings.*

7 a Primary. They were using data in their paper that they had collected themselves.

b *You should have outlined the peer review process shown in Figure B on page 50 in S43.* The paper is sent to the editor of a journal. The editor checks the paper and sends it to scientists working on similar things, who have expert knowledge. The scientists review the paper and then tell the editor whether it should or should not be published and whether or not anything needs changing. The editor then decides whether to publish or not.

8 $\frac{(80 - 9)}{80} = \frac{71}{80} = 0.89$, which is $0.89 \times 100 = 89\%$. *Remember to show your working. That way, you'll get some credit even if you don't get the answer right.*

▮ CRUMBLING MATERIALS

1 a Quantitative. *It contains only numbers.*

b Continuous. *There is a limitless number of other possible values between the values in the data.*

2 a The dependent variable was the mass loss; the independent variable was the amount of sulfur

dioxide.

b Two from:

- mass of stone
- surface area of stone
- amounts of other gases in the air in the container
- temperature
- shape of container
- volume of container.

3 You need to have drawn a scatter graph because you are looking for a correlation (relationship) between two variables that are both quantitative and continuous. Your scatter graph should have:

- a title
- the dependent variable on the *y*-axis – loss in mass. *Remember that in a table, the first column shows the independent variable and the others show measurements of the dependent variable (S30.)*
- the independent variable on the *x*-axis – mass of sulfur dioxide reaching the surface of the rock each day (mg/m^2)
- a good scale for the *y*-axis so that the plotted points are well spread
- a *y*-axis scale that has even divisions
- a *y*-axis scale that is numbered
- a label for the *y*-axis with units
- a good scale for the *x*-axis so that the plotted points are well spread
- a label for the *x*-axis with units
- an *x*-axis scale that has even divisions
- an *x*-axis scale that is numbered
- all points plotted accurately
- all points plotted neatly, with different symbols being used for rock 1 and rock 2
- two lines of best fit – one for each set of points.

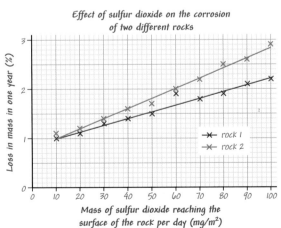

Effect of sulfur dioxide on the corrosion of two different rocks

Loss in mass in one year (%)

Mass of sulfur dioxide reaching the surface of the rock per day (mg/m^2)

4 The reading for rock 1 at 60 mg/m².

5 a Milligrams per metre squared (or milligrams per square metre)

b Compound unit

c Two from:
- to speed up writing things down
- make things look clearer
- things can be understood all over the world no matter what language is spoken.

6 $2(1.5 \times 4) + 2(1.5 \times 4) + 2(4 \times 4) = 56\,cm^2$.
You should show your working even if not asked. And don't forget the units!

7 The sulfur dioxide is a hazard. It can form an acid that can cause injury to skin or eyes; the scientists should avoid breathing this gas in.

8 Repeat the measurements.

9 The more sulfur dioxide that the surface of a rock is exposed to, the more mass it loses.

BIMETALLIC STRIPS

1 3

2 a

Metal	Mean increase in length of 25 cm bar (µm)
aluminium	120
copper	84
gold	70
iron	60
nickel	64
titanium	43
tungsten	23

b To estimate a true value from a range of readings.

c *You need to draw a bar chart because your independent variable is qualitative data. Your bar chart should have:*
- a title
- the dependent variable on the y-axis – mean increase in length
- the independent variable on the x-axis – the metals
- a good scale for the y-axis so that the plotted points are well spread

- a y-axis scale that has even divisions
- a y-axis scale that is numbered
- a label for the x-axis – metals
- a label for each bars on the x-axis – aluminium, iron …
- gaps between the x-axis bars
- an x-axis scale that has even divisions
- all bars plotted accurately
- all bars the same width
- all bars drawn neatly with a ruler

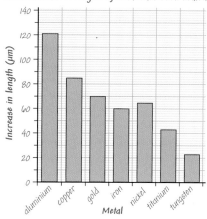
Mean increase in lengths of metal bars when heated

3 *Look at the last column in the table below for the answers. 1 µm is 1000 mm and so to get each value in mm you need to divide them all by 1000.*

Metal	Test 1 (µm)	Test 1 (mm)
aluminium	120	0.120
copper	86	0.086
gold	71	0.071
iron	65	0.065
nickel	66	0.066
titanium	43	0.043
tungsten	25	0.025

4 a

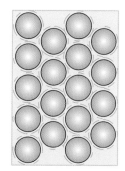
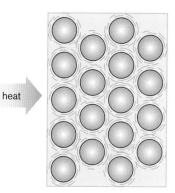
heat

Your model will not look exactly like this but it should have the following features:

- two drawings showing a heated metal and an unheated metal
- the particles in both metals
- the particles in the heated metal moving a greater distance than in the unheated metal
- the same number of particles in both the heated and the unheated metals
- the heated metal taking up more space (expanded) to move
- the particles in both metals being the same size.

b To represent things and make them easier to understand.

5 Aluminium and tungsten; they have the greatest and the least expansion.

6 Gold. *The three readings are all very close together.*

7 **QWC** *The easier way to tackle this is by comparing these results with the check-list on page 49 in S42.*

- *Do the results let you answer the question? (Is the investigation **valid**?)*

Yes. The results let you answer the original question, which was to find out if some common metals expanded by different amounts when heated.

- *Do the results measure what they were supposed to? (Are the actual results **valid**?)*

Yes. Expansion will happen in all directions in a metal bar and so measuring length will provide a measurement of expansion.

- *Were there lots of **anomalous results**?*

No. There were no anomalous results, although the Test 1 result for iron might be considered to be anomalous. The results for iron are not very precise so the tests for iron need to be repeated to be sure.

- *How **repeatable** or **reproducible** are the results?*

The results were all repeatable.

- *Have the results been collected in an unbiased way? (Or is there **bias** in the method that shifts the results in a certain direction?)*

You aren't told many of the details of the experiment so you cannot really answer this. However, it would appear that the results are good.

8 **QWC** All metals expand when they are heated and contract when they are cooled. For example, a 25 cm long aluminium bar gets 120 μm longer when it is heated from 20°C to 40°C. This is because the particles (atoms) that make up metals need more space to move around at higher temperatures.

When two different metals are stuck to one another in a strip, the strip will bend if heated or cooled. Figure A shows this. These strips work because different metals expand and contract by different amounts when heated and cooled.

You might have phrased your answer differently, or made different points. That doesn't matter so long as you have made a point, and then given some evidence to back up your point and explained the link between your evidence and your point.

Glossary

Identifiers	Word	Definition
S16, S23	accuracy	How close a measurement (or set of measurements) is to the real value of something.
S19, S20, S22, S34, S42, S43	anomalous result	A measurement that does not fit the same pattern as other measurements from the same experiment.
S7, S8	area	The amount of surface that a two-dimensional shape covers.
S41, S47, S48	argument	Telling people what you believe and why, usually with reasons why you do not agree with others.
S28	average	A single value that represents all the values in a set of data.
S31, S38	bar chart	Chart showing solid columns that represent data. It is often used when the independent variable is qualitative.
S44	benefit	Something good that could come from an action or device.
S12, S42, S43, S47	bias	If evidence is shifted in a particular direction it shows bias.
S5	categoric data	Data that is not in the form of numbers – also called qualitative data.
S8	circumference	The perimeter or distance round the outside of a circle.
S9	compound measure	A unit of measurement made up of more than one unit – e.g. m/s.
S9	compound unit	See 'compound measure'.
S39, S42, S43	conclusion	A decision made after looking at all the facts.
S5, S30, S32	continuous data	Data in which each value can be any number between two limits.
S14	control	A control uses exactly the same set-up as the main part of the experiment but without the independent variable.
S14	control experiment	An experiment in which a control (or control group) is used.
S14	control group	A control for an experiment that consists of a group of things (usually organisms).
S13, S14, S21, S34	control variable	A variable that needs to be controlled in an experiment, otherwise it will affect the results.
S15	correlation	A link between two variables, so that when one changes so does the other.
S41	counterargument	A reason for not agreeing with an argument.
S41	counterclaim	See 'counterargument'.
S44	criteria	Standards by which things can be judged. The singular is 'criterion'.
S5, S8	data	Numbers, words, etc. that can be organised to give information.

Identifiers	Word	Definition
S27	decimal	A number shown as a single row of digits. There may or may not be a decimal point written in this row. If no decimal point is shown, it is a whole number. If there is a decimal point shown, the digits to the left of it is a whole number and the digits to the right represent fractions.
S27	denominator	The number below the line in a fraction.
S9	density	The mass of a fixed volume of a substance.
S13, S15, S21, S30, S31, S32, S33	dependent variable	A variable that depends on the changes of another variable. This is the variable that you measure in an experiment.
S8	diameter	A line from one side of a circle to the other, passing through the centre.
S35	directly proportional	Two variables are directly proportional if, when one increases then the other increases by the same percentage. This written as $A \, \alpha \, B$.
S5, S30	discrete data	Data in which each value can take only one of a limited choice of numbers.
S44	drawback	Something undesirable that could come from an action or device.
S11, S20	estimate	A rough calculation.
S46	ethics	Actions that a group of people agree are right or wrong. A country's laws are based on ethics.
S42, S43	evaluation	An assessment of how well something does or has done its job.
S4, S5, S8	evidence	Information used to support an idea or show that it is wrong.
S13	factor	See 'variable'.
S13, S21	fair test	An experiment in which all the control variables are successfully controlled so that the only variable that affects the dependent variable is the independent variable.
S13	fixed variable	See 'control variable'.
S1, S38	flow chart	Set of boxes with arrows showing how to move through the steps of a process, including any choices that may need to be made.
S27	fraction	A number shown as two parts with a line between them. The digit below (or after) the line is the total number of possible parts in the whole. The digit above (or in front of) the line is the actual number of parts.
S30, S32	frequency	The number of occurrences of something in a certain time or in a certain area.
S32, S38	frequency diagram	A chart or graph in which the dependent variable is a frequency. A histogram is a specific type of frequency diagram, when groups of continuous data are used for the independent variable.

Identifiers	Word	Definition
S30	frequency table	A table that displays the number of times something happens.
S35	gradient	The slope of a straight line. Calculated by choosing points, and calculating the difference in the values on the y-axis between these two points, and then difference between the two x-values. The gradient is the difference in y divided by the difference in x.
S24, S45	hazard	When something can cause harm.
S32, S38	histogram	A chart showing the frequency of something as a series of bars. Each bar shows a grouped set of data on a continuous scale.
S17	human error	Errors in measurements caused by the people making the measurements.
S3, S4, S39, S40	hypothesis	A scientific idea that can be tested.
S13, S15, S21, S30, S31, S32, S33	independent variable	A variable that does not depend on changes in other variables. This is the variable that you change in an experiment.
S7	index	A small raised number written to the right of another number or unit to show that it should be multiplied by itself, one or more times. The index shows how many of the number are to be multiplied together. The plural is 'indices'.
S7	index form	When an index is shown next to a unit or number, it is said to be in index form – e.g. m^2.
S27	integer	A number that does not contain fractions. Another word for 'whole number'.
S43	journal	Scientific magazine in which papers are published.
S42	justify	Give reasons for.
S4	kinetic theory	Theory based on the idea that all matter is composed of particles that move.
S33, S38	line graph	Graph used to present data in which both the independent and dependent variables are in the form of continuous data. Points are joined together with straight lines.
S34	line of best fit	A straight line drawn through a set of points on a graph so that about half the points are above the line and half are below it.
S20, S28	mean	An average of a set of numbers found by adding them together and dividing by how many there are. A mean lets you estimate the true value of a measurement using repeated measurements.
S47	media	Something through which information travels is a medium. The plural is 'media'.

Identifiers	Word	Definition
S28	median	The middle value, when a set of data values is written out in order.
S28	mode	The most common value in a set of data.
S40	model	Representing a thing or a process in a way that makes it easier to understand. Models usually simplify the real nature of something.
S46	morals	A set of opinions or beliefs agreed by a group about what is right or wrong. A country's laws are based on ethics.
S27	numerator	The number above the line in a fraction.
S41, S46, S48	opinion	What you think about something.
S19, S28, S34	outlier	See 'anomalous result'.
S43, S48	paper	Scientific report written by scientists to tell others about their research. Papers are published in journals.
S43	peer review	Process in which papers are checked by scientists.
S27	percentage	A fraction in which the denominator is 100. Uses the symbol %.
S8	perimeter	The distance round the outside edge of a shape.
S8	pi (π)	The ratio of a circle's circumference to its diameter.
S36, S38	pie chart	Diagram in which the different proportions of something are shown as slices of a circle.
S7	power	See 'index'.
S1, S16, S22, S42	precision	How closely grouped together a set of measurements are.
S3, S39, S40	prediction	Saying what you think an investigation will show.
S9	pressure	The force on a fixed area.
S25	primary data	Data that you collect – e.g. by doing an investigation.
S25	primary evidence	See 'primary data'.
S29	probability	The chance of something happening, shown as a fraction, a decimal or a percentage.
S5, S31	qualitative data	Data that is not in the form of numbers – also called 'categoric data'.
S5, S31, S33	quantitative data	Data that is in the form of numbers.
S8	radius	The shortest distance from the centre of a circle to its circumference.
S12, S29	random	Something that is done without conscious thought and is impossible to predict.
S20, S22, S23	range	The difference between the highest and lowest measured values in an experiment – usually ignoring anomalous results.
S27	ratio	A comparison between two numbers – usually shown in the form x:y.

Identifiers	Word	Definition
S15	relationship	See 'correlation'.
S22	reliable	Results that are repeatable and/or reproducible are said to be reliable.
S21, S22, S42, S43	repeatable	Results that have similar values when repeated by the same experimenter.
S22, S42, S43, S46	reproducible	Results that have similar values when repeated by the different experimenters.
S24, S45	risk	The chance of harm occurring from a certain hazard or drawback.
S11	sample	A small part of a collection of data. Scientists might never collect all the possible data but just collect a sample, which they then use to estimate what the rest of the data is like.
S15, S34, S38	scatter graph	Graph used to look for correlation between two variables. Lines of best fit are often drawn through the points.
S1	scientific method	A series of steps scientists take to show whether a scientific idea is right or wrong.
S25	secondary data	Data that you use but that has been collected by other people.
S25	secondary evidence	See 'secondary data'.
S6	SI system	System of units used by most scientists around the world. SI stands for 'Système International'.
S18, S20	significant figures	The number of digits in a value that show a suitable approximation of the size of that number – all the other digits being replaced by zeros.
S10	standard form	A way of writing very small or very large numbers using a decimal number between 1 and 10 multiplied by a power of 10 – the number 10 with an index.
S30, S38	table	A way of recording data in columns and rows.
S1, S4	theory	A hypothesis (or set of hypotheses) supported by a lot of evidence.
S23	trial run	A cut-down version of an investigation used to work out what measurements to make in the actual investigation.
S21, S39, S42, S46	valid	When something does what it is intended to do it is valid.
S5, S9	value	A number together with something that indicates what the number means (e.g. a unit of measurement).
S13	variable	Something that can change and have different values.
S37, S38	Venn diagram	Diagram composed of enclosed areas that show the associations between different groups.
S7, S8	volume	The amount of space a 3D shape takes up.
S27	whole number	A number that does not contain fractions.

Periodic table

Key

atomic number	relative atomic mass (atomic weight)
1	1
H	
symbol	name
	Hydrogen

Main table (each cell: atomic number, relative atomic mass, symbol, name)

1 1 **H** Hydrogen																	2 4 **He** Helium
3 7 **Li** Lithium	4 9 **Be** Beryllium											5 11 **B** Boron	6 12 **C** Carbon	7 14 **N** Nitrogen	8 16 **O** Oxygen	9 19 **F** Fluorine	10 20 **Ne** Neon
11 23 **Na** Sodium	12 24 **Mg** Magnesium											13 27 **Al** Aluminium	14 28 **Si** Silicon	15 31 **P** Phosphorus	16 32 **S** Sulphur	17 35.5 **Cl** Chlorine	18 40 **Ar** Argon
19 39 **K** Potassium	20 40 **Ca** Calcium	21 45 **Sc** Scandium	22 48 **Ti** Titanium	23 51 **V** Vanadium	24 52 **Cr** Chromium	25 55 **Mn** Manganese	26 56 **Fe** Iron	27 59 **Co** Cobalt	28 59 **Ni** Nickel	29 64 **Cu** Copper	30 65 **Zn** Zinc	31 70 **Ga** Gallium	32 73 **Ge** Germanium	33 75 **As** Arsenic	34 79 **Se** Selenium	35 80 **Br** Bromine	36 84 **Kr** Krypton
37 85.5 **Rb** Rubidium	38 88 **Sr** Strontium	39 89 **Y** Yttrium	40 91 **Zr** Zirconium	41 93 **Nb** Niobium	42 96 **Mo** Molybdenum	43 99 **Tc** Technetium	44 101 **Ru** Ruthenium	45 103 **Rh** Rhodium	46 106 **Pd** Palladium	47 108 **Ag** Silver	48 112 **Cd** Cadmium	49 115 **In** Indium	50 119 **Sn** Tin	51 122 **Sb** Antimony	52 128 **Te** Tellurium	53 127 **I** Iodine	54 131 **Xe** Xenon
55 133 **Cs** Caesium	56 137 **Ba** Barium	57 139 **La** Lanthanum	72 178.5 **Hf** Hafnium	73 181 **Ta** Tantalum	74 184 **W** Tungsten	75 186 **Re** Rhenium	76 190 **Os** Osmium	77 192 **Ir** Iridium	78 195 **Pt** Platinum	79 197 **Au** Gold	80 201 **Hg** Mercury	81 204 **Tl** Thallium	82 207 **Pb** Lead	83 209 **Bi** Bismuth	84 210 **Po** Polonium	85 210 **At** Astatine	86 222 **Rn** Radon
87 223 **Fr** Francium	88 226 **Ra** Radium	89 227 **Ac** Actinium	104 261 **Rf** Rutherfordium	105 262 **Db** Dubnium	106 263 **Sg** Seaborgium	107 262 **Bh** Bohrium	108 265 **Hs** Hassium	109 266 **Mt** Meitnerium	110 269 **Ds** Darmstadtium	111 272 **Rg** Roentgenium	112 285 **Cn** Copernicum	113 286 **Uut** Ununtrium	114 289 **Fl** Flerovium	115 289 **Uup** Ununpentium	116 293 **Lv** Livermorium	117 294 **Uus** Ununseptium	118 294 **Uuo** Ununoctium

Lanthanide series

58 140 **Ce** Cerium	59 141 **Pr** Praseodymium	60 144 **Nd** Neodymium	61 145 **Pm** Promethium	62 150 **Sm** Samarium	63 152 **Eu** Europium	64 157 **Gd** Gadolinium	65 159 **Tb** Terbium	66 162 **Dy** Dysprosium	67 165 **Ho** Holmium	68 167 **Er** Erbium	69 169 **Tm** Thulium	70 173 **Yb** Ytterbium	71 175 **Lu** Lutetium

Actinide series

90 232 **Th** Thorium	91 231 **Pa** Protactinium	92 238 **U** Uranium	93 237 **Np** Neptunium	94 244 **Pu** Plutonium	95 243 **Am** Americium	96 247 **Cm** Curium	97 247 **Bk** Berkelium	98 251 **Cf** Californium	99 252 **Es** Einsteinium	100 257 **Fm** Fermium	101 258 **Md** Mendelevium	102 259 **No** Nobelium	103 262 **Lr** Lawrencium

Index